To Susan *
I just wo
that your g
a second family
Wr thank you for you
and support, Hope you Enjoy
the Book,
[signature]

Dear Susan and Pat,
It is an honor to share
this story with you.
Martin

MANUEL STRONG

The Life and Legacy of James and Florine Manuel

MARTIN S. MANUEL

WESTBOW
PRESS®
A DIVISION OF THOMAS NELSON
& ZONDERVAN

WestBow Press books may be ordered through booksellers or by contacting:

WestBow Press
A Division of Thomas Nelson & Zondervan
1663 Liberty Drive
Bloomington, IN 47403
www.westbowpress.com
844-714-3454

ISBN: 978-1-6642-3766-7 (sc)
ISBN: 978-1-6642-3767-4 (hc)
ISBN: 978-1-6642-3775-9 (e)

Library of Congress Control Number: 2021912600

Print information available on the last page.

WestBow Press rev. date: 06/24/2021

To George Edward Manuel (Uncle George): you were an encourager to us and were together with us, along with your family, on many occasions, snapping many of those 1950–1960 photos that, sadly, we were not able to include in this book. You did the initial work on the family tree that enabled us to know about our ancestors. Thanks for being there!

To Lottie Manuel (Grandma): your love and strength shaped your son, our dad, and you were there for each of us with the special love that only a grandmother can give. Without your caring involvement, our family would not have become what it is today. Thanks for all you did to give birth and support your descendants. You will never be forgotten!

To my sisters and brothers: I credit each of you for your marvelous contributions, without which this book would lack significant content. In your participation, I have come to know, respect, and love each of you more than ever. Thanks, siblings!

Photograph and Art Credits

Written permission to use the photographs in this book has been granted by the following to the author and to the publisher, WestBow Press:

Darion Adams: Chapter 15
Shaquil Adams: Chapter 15
Lauren Adams: Chapter 15
Tyrin Alston: Chapter 15
Rendel Bass: Chapter 15
Reneisha Manuel-Borrero: Chapter 15
Cecilia Jeanette Carter: Chapter 15, 17
Shari Eubanks: Chapter 15
Melanie Fernando: Chapter 15
Nancy Hicks: Chapter 7, 9, 14
Adriene Jones: Chapter 15
Chris Manuel: Chapter 15
Eric Manuel: Chapter 15
Greg Manuel: Chapter 15
Harry Manuel: Chapter 7, 15
Michael Manuel: Chapter 7, 15
Paul Manuel: Chapter 15
Sean Manuel: Chapter 15
Sheena Manuel: Chapter 2, 15
Sherman Manuel: Chapter 7, 11, 13, 15
Tony Manuel: Chapter 11, 15
Tracey Manuel: Chapter 15
Katonyia Parks: Chapter 15
Doreen Ray: Chapter 15
Latosha Reyna: Chapter 15
Janeen Richards: Chapter 15
Janet Richards: Chapter 15

Richelle Williams: Chapter 15
Public domain: Chapter 1, 2
Martin Manuel: All other photos and the maps in Chapter 1, 2
Jinx Manuel donated "Always Do Your Best" to his children.

CONTENTS

Contents

PREFACE

Jared Kushner, senior adviser to President Donald J. Trump, in a late October 2020 interview on Fox News, said, in regard to concerns of black Americans, "President Trump's policies are the policies that can help people break out of the problems that they are complaining about, but he can't want them to be successful more than they want to be successful."

The implication: black people don't want to be successful.

Understandably, Mr. Kushner's comments upset many in the African American community, who considered his statement an expression of the stereotype that black people lack the initiative and effort to improve their economic status. In other words, they are lazy and unintelligent.

Kushner's words represent a common perception among most people in the United States, a blind assumption based on ignorance of four hundred years of American history. Yes, four hundred years of oppression by the majority, many of whom stole their wealth by forcing kidnapped African slaves to serve as the labor pool of their colonization and then, over generations, systematically practiced tactics to hold down these humans already on their backs. Overlooking that historical fact, far too many assume that black people are themselves the cause of their plight and that they are either incapable or unwilling to take steps to improve their condition.

This book tells a different story. It is the real story of a real African American family's rise from slavery and ongoing efforts to hold them back to emerge as a model family of achievers, who, because of their inner strength and faith, would not remain in their imposed condition.

"Manuel strong" is the catchphrase that captures this powerful story about two people, supported by two generations of uprisers from enslavement and poverty. From these two people, blessed by the God to whom they prayed, a legacy of love, parental care, common sense, diligence, intelligence, fortitude, persistence, and unity ensued. They patterned strength for their children, who, being formed in that pattern of strength, replicated it in their children. The result: a unique scene on the American stage.

This book is not about the rise from slavery of one especially gifted person to greatness, such as the *Up from Slavery* story of Booker T. Washington. The *Manuel Strong* story is about ordinary people expressing the desire and drive that God created in them (and all other people because all are made in His image).

The unique aspect of this story is the way that the two heroes, James and Florine Manuel, applied their desire and drive. They did it in love for each other and for their children. This love resulted in their enduring marriage, in spite of assaults against it, and it sparked their devotion to their children—all of them—so that despite the impoverished condition that having many babies brought, they loved those babies, raised them in love, and remained devoted to them and their success in life.

In addition to these things that many other people might have done, James and Florine Manuel, together, reached outside their immediate family to share the desire and drive in them with others around them, especially young people. Regardless of their own limitations of time, they managed to invest time in serving their community.

All of this they did with an underlying fear of God and faith in God. They were not from a lineage of ministers of a religion or even people who outwardly professed religious faith. They simply and sincerely lived their ordinary lives in the fear of and faith in God.

From the outcome, it is obvious that God blessed them. That blessing includes the support given to the Manuel family and individual Manuel children by well-intentioned, good-hearted people, white and black. It includes organizations such as the Catholic charity that helped during a time of economic hardship. All of this took place in a country that, despite its faults, maintains opportunities for its citizens, even if those opportunities are not available on a level playing field.

As descendants of James and Florine Manuel, it is our earnest desire that this story inspires its readers. We hope that this story helps to rewrite the stereotypical history of black families in the United States. We pray that this story serves as a model of what can be in American families. May it strengthen each person in every family, and may it contribute to better communities and a better nation.

1

FROM KENTUCKY TO OHIO

(Time period: 1865–1929)

Kentucky's winters were cold, and its summers were swelteringly hot, like that of other Midwestern states. Though below the Mason-Dixon Line, its climate tended to be more extreme than the states in the Deep South. This was especially felt in the slave houses. Of course, comfort was not expected in the life of a slave in nineteenth-century America. Young and pretty Millie, a fifteen-year-old recently freed girl in central Kentucky, found her life of servitude strenuous, even though her country had declared her free. Legally, she was not a slave, but her work in the house of the Jordan family wasn't much different.

This story of the Manuel family begins just after the Civil War. John Manuel and Millie Beachamp were born slaves but gained their freedom while children. According to the 1870 census, as a teenager, Millie continued to work as a free "domestic servant" for a small family in Hart County, about eighty-five miles south of Louisville. Ten years later, she would be John Manuel's wife, living southwest of Louisville in Breckenridge County, next to the Wimp family, where John had lived as a young slave. The couple had five children—John, James Richard, Hallie, George Lee, and Joseph. Hallie was the lone daughter.

At the same time and same place, the Casey family became part of the story. James Mayfield Casey, known as Jimmie, and Matina Finney-Casey were born slaves in Breckenridge County. Their first child was Edward, who married Matilda Perks in 1890. He, like his father, worked as a farmer. Together, they gave birth to and raised eight children, the first of whom was Lottie in 1892.

The Casey family relocated just north of Breckenridge County, across the Ohio River in Harrison County, Indiana, when Lottie was starting school. Both Edward and Matilda were born after the Civil War in Breckenridge County. Their seven children after Lottie were Sally, Leona, Albert, Raymond, Ruby, Gola, and Mildred. By the time that Lottie was in her mid-teens, the family had returned to Breckenridge, where George Manuel and Lottie Casey were married in 1909. Lottie was a slender and very attractive bronze-skinned young woman with a sweet and gentle personality. She was also strong, as her family faced the difficulties that the twenties, thirties, and forties posed.

George and Lottie had four children while in Breckenridge County. George, a handsome and somewhat stout man with a dark-brown complexion, was remembered by his eldest son, George Edward, as athletic, hardworking, and short-tempered. That temper led to their permanent departure from Kentucky. Young George was around four years of age when his dad came home unusually excited. Soon afterward, when two policemen arrived, it became clear why. He had severely beaten a white man and was about to be arrested. A few days later, he returned to his home, rushing to pack essential items; he was leaving town after another skirmish with law enforcement. He told Lottie that he was unsure where he would go from Louisville, but later, he wrote her from Springfield, Ohio, where he had found a job and settled.

Meanwhile, Lottie and the children had moved in with her parents, Edward and Matilda Casey.

Matina Finney-Casey

Lottie and George Manuel

After the elder George had made arrangements, the whole family, including the Caseys, took the train to Cincinnati and on to Springfield, where they settled on Central Avenue across the street from St. Joseph's Catholic Church. It was 1917, a year after the birth of Cornelius Jesse Manuel, their fourth child. The other three children in birth order were sons George Edward and Cannellee and daughter Zeola. The family did not stay long in that neighborhood. Their street was occupied solely by black people, but a few blocks from there, only white people lived. Fights between the young people in the two groups erupted into serious neighborhood conflicts. To resolve the problem, the city of Springfield evicted all of the black people from their homes.

Strife between white and black people was not as severe in Springfield as it had been in the Louisville area, but the city was segregated, and many business establishments did not cater to (as their signs read) "colored" people.

After several moves, George and Lottie built a home in Springfield's Rosedale area around the time that their fifth child, James William, was born on February 17, 1919.

The family was only in that home for a few years. During the winter of 1923 on a particularly cold day, George tried to thaw frozen pipes with a homemade torch but inadvertently set the attic on fire, causing extensive damage to the house. Neighbors kept the older children for a few weeks while the family relocated to Perrin Avenue.

During those early years in Springfield, George worked in various labor-intensive jobs. He had the reputation of being a hard worker, passing on his work ethic to his children to the extent that they missed out on activities such as swimming, hunting, fishing, and sports games—activities that were common to children their ages.

Lottie served as a homemaker, but she also participated in the construction and finishing of the Rosedale home. Her oldest son, George Edward, told of the accident he caused while he and his mother worked to wallpaper the home; George dropped a board that struck Lottie in the head, knocking her unconscious. Young George found out that his petite mom could express intimidating anger, but after his explanation and apology, she forgave him.

Together, they had come a long way—from the farms that their parents lived on as slaves to independent living with their own home in a town of more tolerance than they had previously known. There, they raised robust, independent children and equipped them to establish strong positions as productive families in their community.

Sadly, Lottie and her husband, George, separated, first temporarily, but by 1930, it was permanent, leaving Lottie to raise the children who were still at home.

After their separation, the two continued to live in Springfield. George, through his diligence and reliability at his workplace, a piano manufacturer, became a foreman at the plant. But as he aged, he was plagued with health problems, including diabetes, resulting in the eventual amputation of the lower half of one of his legs.

Lottie worked at times as a maid, and at other times, she helped family members in various ways. Always, she maintained close relations with her grown children and grandchildren, remaining a sweet person throughout her life.

She outlived George and spent her later years living next door to her sisters, Leona and Sally, along with Leona's husband, Wilton Ford, on West Grand Street in Springfield.

Ironically, the journey of the Manuel and Casey families from Kentucky to Ohio was triggered by a fight. Two strong people, George and Lottie, managed to escape the clutch of restriction that their former home had on them to find freedom and future opportunity for themselves and their posterity.

2

FROM GEORGIA TO OHIO

(Time period: 1840–1929)

South of Louisville, about 560 miles, another story was playing out in the experience of people of African descent in the Deep South in the late-nineteenth and early-twentieth centuries.

March and Maranda Clark, both born slaves in southern Georgia, were parents of five children by 1870, two of whom were twins—Mariah and Mary. March lived to be 105 years old, outliving Maranda and other wives. It is difficult to imagine being born a male slave in the Deep South and living through the Jim Crow experience. March was a strong man to live and endure it for so many years. His strength and longevity did not show up in his daughter Mariah or her daughter Druecilla, but it appeared again in his granddaughter.

March's daughter Mariah was born in 1860 before the Civil War. Her status as a slave ended long before she met Sam Valentine. Although they never married, together they had five children, all daughters; Sam had a son, Lee, by another woman. Records suggest that Sam had been a slave of the Clark family in Houston County, Georgia. The white Clarks and the black Clarks, as well as the Valentines, lived within walking distance of one another. The confusion of Sam Valentine's being father of many children by more than one wife was probably a closely held secret in the early 1900s, and we know even less today.

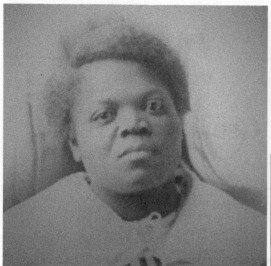

Flanders D. Davis

Josephine Valentine-Davis   Gus Davis

We do know that Mariah and her five daughters resumed using the name Clark for a short time around 1900. In the small village of Perry, about one hundred miles southeast of Atlanta, they lived on the same street as Flanders Davis and several relatives of his mother, Catherine Rutherford, wife of Cornelius Davis. There, Mariah's first daughter, Josephine, met Flanders Davis, and they fell in love. They married, and Josephine gave birth to their first son, Augustus, nicknamed Gus.

Later, Mariah married Sam Varnedoe, who died sometime before 1920. Of the five sisters, only the youngest, Druecilla, had the name Varnedoe. The others carried their maiden names from their father, Sam Valentine. Mariah's new husband, Sam Varnedoe, adopted Druecilla before she reached her teens.

As a widow, Mariah, along with her youngest daughter, Druecilla, lived in the home of Oscar and Mittie Patterson. Mittie was Mariah's second child. She, Druecilla, and their other three sisters, Josephine, Mattie, and Pearl, had split their growing-up years between Cordele, Georgia, and Houston County, Georgia. Cordele is just south of Houston County.

Around 1917, Flanders and Josephine Davis moved from Cordele to Springfield, Ohio, where Flanders had found work while he was preparing to become a church pastor. They brought with them their children, Gus, Lucille, and Flanders Jr. Their new home was a refreshing upgrade from the conditions that they had known in Georgia all their lives. Better jobs were available, and the Davises wasted no time in telling their friends and family members in Georgia about Springfield.

Their enthusiasm prompted Lee Valentine, Josephine's half-brother, to move to Springfield with his wife, Lovie, and their two daughters, Mayme and Pearlie.

In late 1918, while Druecilla was planning to attend college, she became pregnant through her boyfriend, Damascus. Druecilla gave the beautiful baby girl to her older sister, Josephine, who adopted her. Whether the baby's name, Florine, came from Druecilla or Josephine is unknown. Because of the adoption, her last name became Davis. After Florine's birth, Druecilla proceeded to attend Meharry Medical College in Nashville, Tennessee, receiving financial assistance from her sister Mittie, who worked in cotton fields. Druecilla and Damascus did not continue their relationship.

Florine was no more than two years old when Josephine died after a short illness. She and Flanders had decided to give Florine to their oldest son, Gus, along with his wife, Phoebe. Florine grew up as their child.

Gus and Phoebe met in Ohio after his family moved from Georgia. They were married October 8, 1917, in Springfield. Phoebe, born in Kentucky, the daughter of Sanford and Carrie Fisher, was raised by Carrie after the accidental death of Sanford. Later, Phoebe and two of her siblings were raised by Catholic nuns in Cincinnati.

Gus worked as a hotel waiter and, later, for O. S. Kelly Company, a piano manufacturer in Springfield. Phoebe was a homemaker.

In addition to the families of Flanders and Josephine and Lee and Lovie Valentine, others from Georgia moved to Springfield around the same time. Among them were Ed and Mattie Oliver. Mattie was another of Drucilla's sisters. The Olivers and Valentines became neighbors with Gus and Phoebe.

Other relatives of Florine in Springfield included Lucille Davis-Boozer, who Florine called Conluttie. She was the daughter of Josephine and Flanders and the sister of Gus. Also, Flanders Junior was related but not long involved in Florine's life. His son, Gordon, remained close to Florine.

These relatives and their children, especially Flanders Senior, who went by the nickname Love, along with his children, formed a nuclear family around Florine, a family that formed a foundation of love and encouragement for her to live and grow into the beautiful, faith-holding, and strong woman that she turned out to be.

3

THE EARLY YEARS

(Time period: 1930–1948)

James and Florine were two cute little children who grew up to be a beautiful couple: James, brown-skinned and handsome like his dad, and Florine, lighter in complexion and dashingly attractive.

Florine's childhood homes were on Water Street and East Harrison Street in Springfield, where eventually she graduated from Springfield High School. James grew up in several places in the city, two of them near Florine's Harrison Street home. He too attended Springfield High School, but interests in baseball, boxing, and playing the drums led him to quit school before graduation.

In his mid to late teens, James took up amateur boxing and was Springfield Civic AA Lightweight Golden Glove champion in 1937.

Boxing was fun, but his passion was baseball. From the time that he was too young to play, he participated with a men's team as the batboy. A versatile athlete, he could play several positions, but catcher was his specialty.

He and Florine had met early as children, but Florine, known as the pretty little girl in the neighborhood, found that Manuel boy to be a nuisance. He liked her, but his way of expressing affection was teasing and mischief. In her later years of high school, however, Florine became attracted to him. He impressed her as a "hip" drummer in a jazz band, so she found a way to attend his gigs. They fell in love.

Florine and James Manuel in 1945

But her adopted mother, Phoebe, was not equally impressed. She cautioned Florine about James and, to keep tabs on her, insisted on an early curfew. When Florine stayed after a gig to spend time with her boyfriend, and minutes together became hours, she came home very late to find an angry mother waiting. Mama Phoebe whipped Florine with a switch and told her to never let that happen again.

But a switch couldn't dissuade their love.

James struggled financially; gigs with the band were not consistent enough to provide a steady income, so he joined the Civilian Conservation Corps (CCC) camp, a US government program that was part of President Franklin D. Roosevelt's New Deal, providing unmarried young men between ages seventeen and twenty-five with employment in public works. The assignment there was only six months. While there, James proposed marriage to Florine, but Florine did not want to marry while she was still seventeen.

On October 21, 1937, Florine's birthday, they were married. Both of them were eighteen.

At first, they lived for a short time with Lottie in her home on Baltimore Place. Then, they lived, again for a short time, with Gus and Phoebe in their home on Harrison Street. Afterward, they rented an apartment on Foster Street, next door to the house where James previously had lived. There, their first child, Nancy Marie, was born. Almost two years later, Frances Elaine was born.

For a short time, James worked for the Works Progress Administration (WPA), another of President Roosevelt's New Deal programs.

James found a job with the Ohio Steel Foundry. They moved to Baltimore Place. It was now 1942, and the couple's third child, Charles Edward was an infant. Charles was the first New Year's baby of 1942, and for that reason, Florine was awarded prizes by the city of Springfield.

One summer evening Florine put Nancy and Frances to bed and held Charles in her arms while outside talking with a neighbor. The wind was blowing the curtains upstairs where the two girls were asleep. The moving curtains tipped over a kerosene lamp, igniting the floor and curtains. As frightening as it was, the children were rescued without harm, and the fire was put out.

From there, they moved into their first purchased home at 511 Fremont Avenue. The five-room home sold for one thousand dollars. To make the down payment, the couple paid $37.50 a week for ten weeks. The home sat on the edge of a racially segregated neighborhood that was clean and had plenteous children.

At the time of purchase, the house had no electricity; each room had kerosene lamps for light. There was no indoor plumbing. Water was pumped by hand through a faucet on the back porch. The toilet was an outhouse near the back of the property. James and Florine modernized the house, adding electricity and plumbing, making it comfortable and adequate.

Separated from them by a vacant lot, later to be the site of a new elementary school, was Wheldon Park, a former World War II housing development, now occupied solely by low-income white people. This area would later become a challenge to the Manuel children as they grew and learned to cope with the extreme racial hatred of the residents.

The Fremont home was a tremendous step for the family of five, but soon afterward, the couple suffered the loss of their fourth child, Carlotta, who lived less than a month after her birth, dying from complications of dehydration.

In April of the next year, 1944, James enlisted in the Marine Corps. World War II had entered its final stages. James went through basic training and was stationed at Camp Lejeune in North Carolina, but the war ended before he was deployed. He was discharged as a corporal in January 1946.

By that time, Martin Sylvester had been born, and Harry Lee was on the way. James found a job as a janitor at Crowell-Collier Publishing Company. As a pastime, he played semi-pro baseball for the Springfield Tigers.

The team played at Springfield's Memorial Stadium. Martin recalls being there, held by his Grandma Lottie, who sat next to Florine about halfway up in the grandstands and behind home plate. The team players were on the field, and Florine was trying unsuccessfully to get her toddler to recognize his dad; to Martin, all of the players, wearing the same uniform, looked alike. Instead of paying attention to Mom, he was fascinated with the crowd in what seemed to be a gigantic place, unlike anything he had ever seen. His grandma remarked lovingly, "You're so frisky."

Grandma was unforgettable. To Martin, who was born with asthma and frequently needed special care, she was the best! Martin recalls sitting on a potty chair, wheezing and struggling to breathe, with Grandma sitting attentively in front of him. She could do anything, he thought, so he pleaded, "Grandma, make it go away!"

Lottie was a sweet woman, and her presence there in the home was so helpful to Florine that she stayed there for several years. All of the Manuel children recall fondly her birthday gifts, usually one dollar, and the marshmallow cookies she would buy for them. After she moved away, she would mail birthday cards to "Master" or "Miss," followed by the name.

She and her sister Sally Casey helped James and Florine at special times. Sally could not hear or speak, but her keen perception compensated for the disability—something Nancy and Charles found out when they sneaked downstairs in the middle of the night to raid the icebox; Aunt Sally was the only adult at home. The two were startled when she suddenly appeared, shaking her index finger at them about their naughtiness.

Harry's birth after the war and James's return came at a time of relief for the family from the stresses that life had imposed upon them. To the parents' relief, Harry was a healthy baby.

Entertainment in the home primarily came from the radio. Until the oldest children reached their teens, their parents chose the stations. Springfield's two local AM stations were often the choice by day, but at night, the choice was WLAC, Nashville, Tennessee, which played R&B, blues, and some jazz.

In 1948, Drucilla Florine was born. The choice of the name Drucilla, nicknamed Googie, coincided with the reconnection between Florine and her biological mother (detailed in the next chapter).

Until around 1951, there was an upright piano in the living room. Neither parent played, but James liked to pick out tunes. Martin, before he entered school, was attracted to it and quickly learned to play by ear. But there was no money for formal training, and because of wear and tear, the piano was removed.

The drums were James's instrument in the band he played in as a teenager. Occasionally, as an adult, he would take his drum set to a gig with local jazz bands. His musical talent included composing songs, but he never attempted to publish them. Instead, he and Florine would entertain the children by singing, in harmony, two of their favorites of his compositions: "My Dear" and "This Is Just Out of This World." To this day, the older children still have memories of these tunes, and on one of the birthday celebrations late in Florine's life, they sang them with her.

The younger children were less exposed to this part of their parents' talents, but years later, when they were still preteens, they would laugh as they heard:

"Ann and Jan, Jan and Ann, Ann and Jan, Jan and Ann, Ann and Jan are part of the clan ..."

"Michael, Michael, Michael is my pick; Michael, Michael Dominic ..."

"Chris, Chris, Chris, he's a fine little fellow. Chris, Chris, Chris, that cat he's real mellow ..."

Picking up on the trend, one of the children composed: "Paul, Paul, will you be a Beatle? Paul, Paul, will you be a pope ..."

That was in the sixties.

Returning to the early years, singing together was a pastime for the family. They sometimes spent hours together, harmonizing, playing drum rhythms on oatmeal boxes, and sharing laughs.

The early years were full of fun but empty of cash. It was with this backdrop that something wonderful arose on the stage of the United States of America. The story that emerged defies expectations, demonstrating what can be when there is faith, hope, and the strength to relentlessly pursue a vision of doing the best in life, against all odds, overcoming opposition, and persevering to the end.

4

REACQUAINTANCE WITH GEORGIA

(Time period: 1948–1950)

Learning that you are adopted and that your parents are not the people who conceived and bore you can come with inexpressible reactions. Florine did not discuss her reactions; that is, not with her children.

Flanders and Josephine Davis and, later, Gus and Phoebe Davis loved that beautiful baby and child they raised together. That love meant everything to Florine, contributing to her wholeness and fitness as a human being, as well as her devotion to her own children—to bear them and raise them—seventeen times! Regardless of the details woven through her life, having seventeen babies says everything about the strength that she brought to the Manuel family.

Florine knew about her roots in Georgia, having heard about them during her childhood, but until she reached her late twenties, she had not met her biological mother or other family members who still lived there. That changed in 1948, when Edward Spence, then a fourteen-year-old, along with his cousin Bobby Trigg, visited Edward's half-sister Florine in her home.

Druecilla Spence, Edward's mother—now a widow, as her husband, Cyril Spence, had died a year earlier—reached out to her daughter for the first time and invited her and her family to visit in Atlanta.

The trip by train took place in 1950, with Florine and James traveling together with all of their children. The fascinating sound of the steam locomotive, its whistle, and the clickety-clack of the wheels on the tracks lingered for many years in some of their minds. *Chug-a-chug-chug-chug, chug-a-chug-chug-chug, waah-waahooo-wahooooo, chug-a-chug-chug-chug*—endlessly.

They arrived in Atlanta and were picked up in a limousine. They rode along Peachtree Street, passing beautiful homes along the way, and arrived at what seemed to be a mansion—Druecilla's home.

Except for a slight difference in complexion (Druecilla was slightly darker), there was a strong resemblance between Druecilla and her daughter, Florine. Druecilla noted that Frances looked like the family of Florine's biological father.

To ordinary people on the lower part of the income spectrum, it was astonishing to sit at a large table and be served by apron-wearing attendants. The older children found it rewarding to tell everyone they saw that they were Mrs. Spence's grandchildren. Sodas at the pharmacy were free to them. Southern culture was evident with grits with breakfast, lunch, and supper.

Druecilla, who had graduated from Meharry Medical College with a pharmacy degree, owned and managed Spence's Pharmacy in Atlanta. Also, she owned other properties, including a large country estate northeast of the main business district. There, she employed a group of cotton farmers. She and her late husband, Cyril, who served as a dentist for about twenty years in Atlanta, were wealthy and well known. A book about prominent black people in Atlanta through its history of racial abuse and discrimination, *Courage to Dissent: Atlanta and the Long History of the Civil Rights Movement*, by Tomiko Brown-Nagin, records on page 124 a successful lawsuit filed by C. A. Spence and his wife against the city of Atlanta's streetcar company for racial abuse. That side of the family exhibited its own courage and fighting spirit against oppression.

There, at her large estate with multiple buildings, with the extra-wide concrete driveway closed off by a single-hinged metal gate, was a large house—a mansion to the eyes of ordinary people. Living on the premises with Druecilla were her niece Gussie Bell Davis-Trigg and Gussie's son, Bobby, along with Edward.

The older Manuel children recall some mischievous events that they attributed to those two boys, one in which a box of firecrackers was placed on a heat register; another in which a person with a sheet over the head lurked hauntingly in the Jack-and-Jill bathroom between one bedroom and another where Nancy and Frances slept.

It was not clear exactly how many people lived with Druecilla; besides Gussie Bell, others were there. Nancy and Frances recall that, as children, they felt unwelcome by those adults who lived with Druecilla. It seemed to them that these relatives were not at all interested in Druecilla's plan.

Druecilla wanted Florine and James to move to Atlanta. On one day during their visit, she arranged for them to be driven in her limousine to view one of the properties that had a home and acreage, offering them the property and offering James the supervisory position at the cotton farm. Frances, by then a pretty ten-year-old, became Druecilla's darling, and her biological grandmother imagined and even hinted at raising her as her own and putting her through college.

James did not hide his disinterest in either idea. Even with the financial advantages, he considered raising his children in the South a step backward for the family. He and Florine told Druecilla that they could not accept her offer, an act that probably offended her. After they returned home, Florine did not hear from her mother again.

Florine did not hear again from Edward either, but Arthur Davis, father of Gussie Bell, who lived with Druecilla, visited Florine from time to time to, he said, see how she was doing. Florine suspected that he might have been checking up on her on behalf of Druecilla.

Arthur was the brother of Flanders Davis and was married to the former Pearl Valentine, one of Drucilla's sisters.

The encounter with her biological mother was informative but left an emotional scar on Florine. Despite the wealth that Druecilla enjoyed in her lifetime, she died with nothing, having spent her last years in a nursing care facility in Upstate New York. She left nothing in her will for her daughter, who, with a large family, could have used an inheritance, if only a small part of Druecilla's former possessions. Instead, according to one of Florine's distant relatives still living in Georgia, so-called friends or relatives siphoned off all that Druecilla had earned.

In 1969, Florine traveled to Poughkeepsie, New York, joining a small number of other relatives to bury her biological mother.

As for her biological father, although Florine never knew him, there were rumors about his prosperous life as a medical doctor. Records available today suggest that the man suspected to have been her father graduated from Lincoln University in Philadelphia and subsequently became a prominent heart surgeon, with a practice in Philadelphia. There, he married and arranged for his parents from Georgia to join him, but in the prime of his life, the mid-1950s, he died unexpectedly.

He has a living son, who would be Florine's half-brother. Although some of the Manuel children have visited him in his home in southern Virginia and believe that he might be their uncle, there has been no confirmation.

Edward went on to serve in the US Army, fighting in Vietnam, where his valor earned him the Bronze Star and the Purple Heart, awarded in 1971.

He was married and has living children, but there has been no contact between them and Florine's family. His death occurred in 1994 in Michigan.

5

A GROWING FAMILY

(Time period: 1948–1956)

Arriving back from Georgia, James and Florine settled into what was, in retrospect, their big job: producing a large family.

By then, they already had six children: Nancy, Frances, Charles, Martin, Harry, and Drucilla.

Life around the home was busy, but the parents were young, energetic, and up to the task. There was, however, an ongoing financial challenge. To meet it, James took on additional jobs. Besides his full-time, second-shift janitor job at the Crowell-Collier plant, he took any part-time job that he could. Many of these involved janitorial-type work on a smaller scale, such as at a restaurant, a nightclub, a stadium, or a bowling alley. Sometimes, he would take his young sons with him to help. He became a pin-setter at a bowling alley before automatic pin-setting machines replaced human pin-setters. Charles, by then a young teenager, was his right-hand man.

At the Fremont Avenue home, James made the most of the property, planting fruit trees and a grapevine and building a large shed at the back of the property. He raised chickens, erecting an incubator in his cellar that enabled hatching, even in the cold of winter. He acquired hunting dogs to accompany him on hunting trips to bring home freshly killed game on special occasions. Again,

Charles was his companion; when Martin reached the age to fill in, his asthma usually prevented his taking that role.

As a young father, James understood the value of including his children in his activities. An example is the shed project. When Martin was five years old, he was watching his dad build a shed. Suddenly, James said, "Martin, come here and hold this board." The board was perhaps six feet long and heavy, and there was no way that the small boy could hold the board, but his dad involved him and made him think that he was doing something important. Then, after nailing the board in place, James said, "Good job, Martin," filling the boy with pride and warming him to his daddy.

The shed James built was large. Part of it served as a chicken hutch, and the other part was for coal storage. He built an access window to the alley behind the shed so that coal delivery trucks could easily unload directly into the shed. His work often showed innovation and careful thought.

Meanwhile, Florine did everything involved in mama-type supervision, keeping house, and meal preparation. She started including Nancy and Frances in the kitchen, and before long, they were preparing some meals. Their help became even more necessary every two years (or more frequently), when Florine was giving birth to and caring for another baby.

Early on, James and Florine learned that training their children and giving them freedom and opportunities came with risks. One such experience occurred with Nancy, who, at around ten years of age, was allowed to do work for the next-door neighbor, Mrs. Crowe. Nancy spent considerable time in this neighbor's house, doing chores, even when Mrs. Crowe wasn't there. She invited her young helper to eat whatever she found in the icebox.

One day, Nancy's eyes lit up when she found a cake, fully baked and iced but uncut. Following up on the invitation, she enjoyed a slice. Later, Mrs. Crowe came in and was upset to see a slice cut from the cake she had baked for a special occasion.

Nancy knew she was in trouble; she could never explain to

her parents that she did not intend to steal the cake, so she ran away, fearing what she would face. About a mile or so from home, a cousin noticed her walking along a street where she would not normally walk. He brought her to his home, and his parents did the rest, taking her back to her worried parents. Nancy was punished but realized that running away was not the solution to making a mistake. Lesson learned.

After the return from Atlanta, Gregory Franklin was born. He was called Greg ever since. Two years later, twins—Sheena Virginia and Sherman Douglas—were born. The next year, it was James Anthony, nicknamed Tony. Florine was slow to recover after his birth.

Now the family was up to ten children. Of course, it didn't stop there, but over the years, the number at home did not swell much above that number because about the time a new baby was born, one of the older children moved away from home.

Although the work around the house seemed endless, it was not all work. "Deddy," as the children called James, played with them as if he too was a child—all types of childhood games, such as tag, hide-and-seek, dodge ball, card games, and Monopoly and other board games, as well as bowling in the house. He built a beautiful miniature wooden bowling alley, complete with balls and pins. He bought plastic pins and balls and organized bowling games in what was called "the middle room," the place where the family spent time together when indoors.

Most of the playing, however, was outdoors in the backyard. James taught all of his children how to play baseball. There was not always a real baseball or bat available, so they used whatever they could—a well-carved stick and a makeshift ball out of rubber or even a cast-away baby doll's head. These games attracted neighbor kids, so the Manuel backyard became like a neighborhood playground.

Nearby children and friends of the Manuel children hung around the Manuel house because that was where the fun was. They joined in the family games. Sometimes, the bigger boys pretended to be friends with Charles, but they really wanted to be around Nancy and Frances. During the summer, some of these kids only went home at night to sleep and were back the next day. Florine stretched the meals to include these kids. Often, she would say that it was better for their children to be home, even if other kids were consuming their scarce food. Another comment she and James would make was that they loved keeping neighbor children out of trouble. James and Florine were amazingly unselfish.

Nancy and Frances, along with their friend Dorothy Bronston, enjoyed singing together and dreamed of being a famous trio, like the McGuire Sisters. Several other girls, friends of Nancy and Frances, would spend most of their days around the Manuel home, especially during the summer. Cooking was a big thing for the girls; they helped Florine with meals and baking biscuits, making jelly and scrumptious cobblers, and baking all kinds of pies.

"Mama," as Florine was called, played in some of the games too, when she was not busy caring for a baby or too far along in a pregnancy to risk playing. Of the two parents, she was more like an adult and tended to keep an adult demeanor around the children.

Florine included the children in the responsibilities of the home. Besides teaching Nancy and Frances to cook, she also taught them to care for the babies and toddlers. Nancy would escort the younger children to the outhouse. Frances loved to rock the babies. First, there was a rocking chair, but after it was gone, she rocked, or "bumped," them in an ordinary straight chair. She could bump them for hours as she listened to her favorite music on the radio. Florine kept up with teaching and the distribution of responsibilities as each of the older children grew and was able to help around the house.

Where did these parents find time to do these things?

It seems that in the first twenty years of their marriage, the couple never took time for themselves. All of their time was shared with the children. To them, it was not a chore; they loved doing things with their children, and doing so became their pastimes.

Where did they find the time to make more babies? That was their secret.

Make no mistake; the Manuel home was more than work and play. Obviously, when that many children are in the same place, there is chaos—all the time! The house could never stay neat.

James and Florine were excellent parents. They did not attend a child-rearing class, but they were raised by parents who practiced discipline, and the couple applied the lessons they learned from their parents. They taught their children to show respect to all adults and answer them with "Yes, ma'am" or "No, sir."

James was the primary disciplinarian. He was, as James Brown put it, the "Papa Don't Take No Mess" man of the house. He loved his children and had lots of fun with them, but he taught them appropriate behavior: respect, obedience, and fairness to each other. Never were they to lie, and never were they to fight each other.

He was not an abuser, and he did not enjoy punishing a child, but he understood the necessity of maintaining strict discipline. Every Manuel child knew that if their behavior got out of line, it would be confronted. Everyone disliked getting a "whippin'," as they called it. Deddy would use a belt on a bigger child; smaller children got the switch. There were even times when they had to go outside and pick their own switches. Only the back side was struck, but it hurt and taught important lessons.

Florine punished a little less consistently and not as firmly, but she was no pushover. All the children dreaded her saying, "I'm going to tell your dad when he gets home."

The two were always supportive of each other. There was no way for a child to manipulate one of them into getting on his or her side. Disrespecting one parent meant getting into trouble with the other.

Part of their teaching style emphasized a strong work ethic. If a child was told to wash the dishes, mop the floor, or make the bed, usually the order was followed by an inspection. A common expression of the parents was, "I thought I told you to ..." It was spoken as a question but with a slight frown. The child's response usually was, "I did." Then, whatever the task, the parent would say, rather humorously, "You *opped* the floor," altering the word by omitting the first letter. Snickering, Deddy or Mama would then show by example what they intended and tell the child to do it over again. It effectively taught that a job is to be done well. They knew when to say, "Good job" and said it quite often.

Neither of them was highly educated, so scholastic teaching was not their forte. They expected passing grades in school but not necessarily high performance. Nonetheless, they understood the differences in their children's talent levels and tended to expect more from and encourage the more talented. Their speech tended to be clear so, by example, the Manuel children spoke clearly and appreciated proper grammatical expression.

Common sense was their strength. They would teach their children: "Everyone puts their pants on one leg at a time"; "You can do anything as well as somebody else does"; "If someone irks you on the job, never respond by punching; you will become the problem and lose your job"; and, most notably, "If you want to be accepted as equal, you must be better." These principles and others stuck with the children and guided them through their lives as they grew up and experienced personal challenges.

The parents were flexible with their children in allowing them, if not encouraging them, to be who they were, although each child was very different from the others and their parents.

Nancy and Charles seemed to enjoy pushing the envelope, always overstepping the boundaries of permissibility. Frances loved to dream of travel, wanting to visit and even live in exotic places. Charles was given the opportunity to spend summers with his uncle in Dayton to play for his baseball team. Martin was curious about the operation of electronic things; he enjoyed opening the covers of the radios and the TV, scaring his parents about the danger of electricity. Harry loved sports, following James in baseball and pursuing his own interests too. He was a uniquely gifted ambidextrous athlete who seemed to play everything well. Drucilla liked to make rhymes and tunes and later showed an artistic talent.

These were some of the unique expressions of the older members of the family. Diversity would explode as the family grew, as we shall see as the story continues.

In the late 1940s and early 1950s, radio dramas captivated the family's interest after supper and before bedtime. *The Greatest Story Ever Told* and *Hopalong Cassidy* were two programs they enjoyed.

By the mid-1950s, television was a growing favorite for in-home entertainment. James and Florine purchased their first TV during that time and placed it in the living room. The TV was a Philco tabletop black-and-white model with a rooftop antenna for reception. Sports, such as Cincinnati Reds baseball, Cleveland Browns football, and professional Friday night boxing were James's preference. Florine liked the daytime soap operas. Family favorites included *Lassie*, cartoons, and westerns.

After James got his first car, a used 1948 black Dodge sedan, Sunday afternoon was a time for the whole family to pack into the front and back seats of the vehicle for a ride, with those on the seats holding one or two others on their laps. With windows down and the breeze blowing through the car, James would head for one of the country roads outside of Springfield, where the hills along the road were closely spaced. Traveling at fifty miles per hour, cresting one of those hills and then dropping on the other side felt like a roller coaster, sparking extended exclamations of "Oh!" from everyone in the car. When the car started to climb up the next hill, the vehicle was filled with laughter until, suddenly, there was the next drop. In those days, there were few cars on the road, so a collision was highly unlikely.

Christmas was a special time for everyone but especially the Manuel children. In early December, the house would begin to sway with the sound of Christmas carols, sung mostly by the children, with the older ones taking the lead and teaching the young ones. At times, the children would sit side by side on couches and chairs, rocking or bumping as they sang. There was always a decorated Christmas tree in the living room. Under it were a small number of presents until Christmas morning, when the parents awoke the children long before dawn to open their gifts. To all the children's amazement, there were many more gifts under and all around the tree. Where James and Florine got the money to purchase the prodigious number of gifts—usually at least three per child and some as elaborate as bicycles—is a mystery to this day.

The family—now with eleven children at home, spanning in ages from one year to seventeen years—was young, vibrant, healthy, and stable. As the mid-1950s set in, however, changes and challenges to the family's health and stability would take place.

6

HARDSHIP

(Time period: 1957–1959)

Crowell-Collier Publishing Company had a large printing and publication facility in Springfield that employed several thousand people. James had worked for the company for about ten years as a janitor, but in 1956, after Christmas, the company abruptly announced that it would close its Springfield plant.

The news was a shock to everyone.

As one of the largest employers in a city of eighty thousand people, the plant closing had a devastating impact on the city and its residents, many of whom faced financial disaster. The Manuel family was one such casualty. Because of the glut of available employees seeking work in other companies, the huge job loss made finding replacement jobs extremely difficult. James was out of work for about a year. With unemployment income insufficient to pay the family expenses, James and Florine looked for any available solutions.

James, who often worked a second and even third job part time while employed by Crowell, found additional part-time work that helped, but his total income was still significantly below their needs. Florine sought help through the Catholic Church, which she had attended since a child. The church, through its nuns—"Sisters

Convent"—donated weekly vouchers for bread and milk. Florine worked at home on the church's laundry for additional income.

During those months, every member of the family suffered from hunger. Meals were as economical as possible, and second helpings were not available. The older boys went to the convent once each week to pick up the vouchers, and Florine sent them to the local dairy and bakery to exchange them for bottles of milk and loaves of bread.

Occasionally, charity groups would bring baskets of canned food, fruit, and other food items. There was no meat, but somehow, Florine managed to have a little fish, usually salmon patties, available each Friday, according to Catholic tradition.

James hunted for wild game during hunting season. Thanksgiving and Christmas would always be big dining occasions, with rabbit or pheasant from the hunt and donated turkey. Scarce as food was, Florine and the girls always made the meals delicious. The turkey stuffing was memorable.

The children went to extra lengths to help. Sherman, a first-grade student at Lincoln Elementary School, asked his teacher if he could have the Christmas tree that was in the classroom. The school was about to close for the Christmas break, so the teacher told him yes, not knowing that Sherman had intentions to immediately take it home. While she was out of the room, the little boy dragged the tree from the school building for the two-block walk home. But snow had begun to fall and was accumulating, making his walk and haul all the more strenuous. About halfway home, Sherman, cold and tired, sat down in the snow in a churchyard and dozed off. At home, Harry missed his brother and decided to look for him, walking straight to the churchyard. There, he found his brother lying on the ground. The two of them, with the damaged tree, made it home, and that Christmas, when the family had not been able to afford a tree, they proudly set up Sherman's tree in the living room.

In about a year, James found a steady job, working for the city of Springfield's Street Repair. The smell of asphalt in his work clothes each day was nothing sweet, but it was a reminder of how hard he worked to support his family. Later, he worked for the city's Trash Collection Department.

Slowly, in the late 1950s, the family emerged from the need for charitable assistance.

This short period in the family's history illustrates two things that are important to mention: First, we see the resiliency of the family. No one capitulated in the face of hardship. The parents' priority was the care of their children. The children remained calm and trusting in their parents' care. Second, we see that charitable assistance is essential at times. The empty cupboard and refrigerator posed a far greater threat than slight malnutrition; the children actually faced starvation or severe illness caused by malnourishment. Poverty is not always caused by personal failure. Sometimes, even hardworking people can encounter financial failure. Recipients of charitable contributions or government subsidies are not lazy and are not necessarily single-parent households.

The best part of this episode in the story of the Manuel family was that it was short. They survived, and they understand the debt of gratitude they owe to those who compassionately helped.

7

BIG ONES AND LITTLE ONES

(Time period: 1956–1969)

By the mid-1950s, three of the Manuel children were teenagers. Nancy and Frances were in high school. With a house full of children, preteen down to infant, James and Florine had to distinguish between their growing crop of children and the roles that they would play in the family.

The concept of "big ones" and "little ones" came from this need. More was expected of the big ones; they had more responsibilities but also greater freedoms. The big ones were to look out for and care for the little ones.

Nancy, Frances, and Charles were the first to be considered big ones. By the late 1950s, Martin and Harry were added.

On August 20, 1955, Nancy and her boyfriend, Rendal Bass, were married. Nancy was a fabulously beautiful seventeen-year-old bride. She and her new husband, who was nineteen, rented a house on Fremont Avenue about a block from the family home. Early the next spring, their first child, Shari Renee, was born.

By that time, Florine had given birth to Michele Diana, making eleven Manuel children, ten at home. And Florine was not through with childbearing. In fact, over the next three years, while Nancy added three more children—Katonyia Marie, Adriene Ann, and

Tyrin Raynetta—Florine kept pace by adding Theresa Annette, Cecelia Jeanette, and Michael Dominic. Theresa and Cecelia, who we called by their middle names, Annette and Jeanette, were twins.

Nancy

Frances

All of these children were healthy. Other than typical (at the time) childhood illnesses, such as measles, mumps, and chicken pox, which swept through the family in several stages, there were no serious ailments, except polio, which was detected early in Charles and successfully treated, and asthma in Martin from birth until he reached his mid-teens.

Charles

The Manuel children attended both public and private schools. Nancy and Frances started their elementary education in St. Raphael Catholic School but later transferred to Frey Elementary School. St. Raphael School was difficult for Nancy, not for academic reasons but for the harassment she experienced from other students, as well as problems that she encountered with the school administration. Charles and Martin started in public school at Frey Elementary School. That school was over a mile from the Manuel home, but Lincoln Elementary School was only a few blocks away. The assignment of Fremont Avenue children to Frey effectively segregated the two schools. James and Florine voiced their opposition to the school assignments, and the Springfield school system eventually adjusted the assignments.

Charles and Martin transferred to Lincoln Elementary School, and Harry started there. One year later, a new Lincoln Elementary School opened only a block away from the Manuel home. There, Drucilla, Greg, Sheena, Sherman, and Tony also attended. Nancy, Frances, Charles, Martin, Harry, and Drucilla continued in public schools, going on to Hayward Junior High and Springfield High School, later named Springfield South High School.

In 1959, Frances graduated from Springfield High School.

Earlier that same year, on March 16, 1959, George Lee Manuel, who was James's father and "Papa Manuel" to the children, died. He had suffered from diabetes and for a while walked on a peg leg after an amputation.

After James and Florine had been married over twenty years, having devoted virtually every waking minute of their time to the care and development of their children, at last, because the big ones were taking on increased responsibilities in the care and development of the little ones, the now-middle-aged parents began to find ways to spend time together without the children.

In 1960, Christopher Eugene, nicknamed Chris, was born, and Frances moved into an apartment in Springfield; about a year later, Charles joined her there. The two were there for a year or so when Frances, having completed on-the-job medical training in assisting nurses and administration, moved to Los Angeles for a job opportunity in the medical field; Charles joined her shortly afterward.

In 1962, Martin graduated from Springfield South High School and enrolled in RETS Technical School in Dayton, graduating a year and a half later with a diploma in electronics technology.

On June 6, 1963, Phoebe Davis, called "Big Mama" by the Manuel children, died of leukemia. Before the end of summer, James and Florine agreed to move the family to Harrison Street to be closer to "Big Daddy," Gus Davis. It was after this move that Greg, Sheena, Sherman, and Tony transferred to St. Joseph Catholic School, where Michele, Annette, Jeanette, and Michael also attended.

By this time, the big ones were Martin, Harry, Drucilla, and Greg. The little ones were Sheena, Sherman, Tony, Michele, Annette, Jeanette, Michael, and Chris. Paul Augustus was born in 1964, the youngest of the seventeen children.

The big ones imitated what they had seen in their parents, being deeply involved in the lives of the little ones—playing with them, teaching them sports, and encouraging their development. This freed James and Florine to increase their time with each other outside the home; they joined a bowling league and participated with friends their age in social activities.

In 1965, Martin moved into an apartment in Springfield, and Harry graduated from Springfield South High School, where he had excelled in baseball and wrestling.

In 1966, Martin moved to Chicago for a job opportunity, and Harry enlisted in the US Marine Corps. That same year, the dream that James had of living in the country came to fruition when he and Florine decided to purchase a home near Urbana, Ohio, on Middle Urbana Road.

Family in Urbana

Martin

Harry

Drucilla

The move was refreshing for the entire family. James retired from coaching baseball teams (his baseball activities are covered in a later chapter). He raised hogs and planted a garden. The country atmosphere sparked healthy growth in the children, and the Urbana school system offered them new opportunities, both academically and in sports. Greg, Sheena, Sherman, Tony, Michele, Annette, Jeanette, Michael, Chris, and Paul all completed their schooling in Urbana schools: St. Mary Catholic School and Urbana Public Schools, graduating from Urbana High School.

At the same time, the older Manuel children were adding new members, generating a multitude of offspring of James and Florine. These will be discussed in detail in a later chapter, but one is worth mentioning here. In February 1966, Sean Christopher was born to Charles and his girlfriend in California. A little later, James and Florine agreed to adopt Sean.

In 1967, Drucilla graduated from Springfield South High School.

In 1967, Harry was deployed to Vietnam for one year to fight in the war. He became the first since his father to wear the uniform, and he was the first to be involved in active combat outside of American soil. No doubt, his exposure to the dangers of this conflict, in which American soldiers were dying daily or being captured as prisoners of war, was a source of considerable worry for his parents. But they did not transfer their worries to their children.

In 1968, Martin married Genneen Whisonant, whom he had met in Chicago, and the couple lived in Harvey, Illinois, a nearby suburb.

Harry was discharged from the Marines in 1969 and moved to California, enrolling in a community college to study accounting.

By this time, the big ones were Greg, Sheena, Sherman, Tony, and Michele. The little ones were Annette, Jeanette, Michael, Chris, Paul, and Sean.

The Manuel children, like their parents, were all attractive. Some had features from their mother's side, which included a lighter skin complexion. Some had a darker complexion like their father's, and they, like many black children growing up in a culture inordinately race-and color-conscious, took on feelings of inferiority because of their skin color, even though they came from the same parents. One of the Manuel girls recognized this trait in herself; she realized that her shyness stemmed from her belief that she was not pretty because she was dark skinned. Sadly, that misconception pervades all levels of American society.

James and Florine did not draw attention to the differences in their children's skin color. Instead, they did their best to convey a racially neutral frame of mind in all that they did. James was ahead of his time in Springfield, particularly in his work with boys, having racially integrated teams. (More is explained on this in the next chapter.)

Throughout the years, after James and Florine married up to the mid-1960s, James played baseball or coached baseball teams. As we proceed in the story of this family, we next will look in detail at his involvement in the sport and its effect on the family.

8

BASEBALL

(Time period: 1935–1965)

James loved baseball. He had a slogan that he would use when he was coaching boys about the game: "Eat, drink, and sleep baseball."

He was an outstanding player. Those who knew him in his younger days often commented that had Major (or Minor) League Baseball allowed African American players when he was in his prime, he would have been a Major League player.

Everybody knew him as Jinx, but it wasn't a negative effect that he had on opposing teams that mattered; it was how good he was as a player and later as a coach. He knew the sport inside and out. He knew fundamentals of catching, throwing, hitting, pitching, fielding, bunting, and even in drawing a walk. He was not a fast runner, but he knew how to run the bases. Every great baseball player knows that running bases is a special skill, and that skill lies in the brain. That's why Jinx was a genius in every aspect of the game.

He started playing as a young boy and continued as a young man before World War II. After the war, he played for the Crowell-Collier men's team in the late 1940s, and he went on to play semi-pro baseball for the Springfield Tigers, a Negro League team equivalent to today's Major or Minor League. His primary position was catcher.

Long after his prime days and into his forties, Jinx continued to play on and coach a men's team. When he played, he often had the highest batting average on the team.

Mostly, though, after he turned thirty, Jinx coached. He liked most to coach teenage boys. Often, he was heard saying that his intent was to give boys something to do "to keep them out of trouble."

Post-war youth baseball in Springfield was organized as a Sandlot League. Teams were categorized as Pre-Cub (twelve- to thirteen-year-olds), Cub (fourteen- to fifteen-year-olds), Junior (sixteen- to seventeen-year-olds), and Senior (eighteen-year-olds). Throughout much of the 1950s, Jinx coached teams in all categories. Springfield youth baseball teams were mostly racially segregated, but Jinx defied the norms by having racially integrated teams. Year after year, his teams dominated their opponents. At least five times, he took one of his teams to the national Knothole Baseball Tournament in Cincinnati. In 1961, his team won the national championship in the Pre-Cub division.

When Little League arrived in Springfield, Jinx got involved, coaching teams from 1955 through 1965. From 1958 on, his team was league champion. His team won the city tournament four times. Six Manuel boys played Little League Baseball; five of them played for their dad. After the family moved to Urbana, they discontinued participation in Little League Baseball but not sports.

James's skill at coaching demonstrated his gifted teaching ability, which he also demonstrated as a father. He used baseball to teach about life. Through competition, he taught sportsmanship, effort, playing smart, fairness, honesty, humility, and teamwork.

He was most interested in teaching his children, but through his civic-mindedness, he shared the lessons with any kid who wanted to learn.

In 1964, James wrote a poem titled "Always Do Your Best"[1] for his children. This poem exemplified his philosophy of life.

---

[1] "Always Do Your Best" was neither copyrighted nor published; James donated it to his children.

Always Do Your Best

Do your best if it's work or play,
Do your best no matter what they say,
To do your best may not always be fun,
But you can succeed in the long run.
Always do your best.

Do your best, stand straight and tall,
To answer the challenge whenever it calls.
To be able to stand pressure and pain,
Whenever your body is filled with pain.
Always do your best.

Do your best, lose if you may,
Do your best, for tomorrow is another day.
To suffer defeat is no sin,
Do your best, and tomorrow you can win.
Always do your best.

Do your best with all your might,
And keep the top within your sight,
Don't be afraid, you have nothing to hide,
Only you and God know how hard you tried.
To always do your best.

—Jinx Manuel

His baseball playing and coaching modeled the words of that
poem. His children knew that he lived by those words in everything

he did. The words became a mainstay for many of them as they went through life experiences as adults.

Steve Williamson was one of the boys whom Jinx coached in Little League. From the time that Steve was eight and each year afterward through twelve, Jinx coached him to become one of the city's best Little League players. Steve went on to become a doctor of psychology in Boston, Massachusetts. Over twenty years later, he wrote a letter to his former coach and published the letter for others to read. The following is an excerpt of that lengthy article titled "Jinx Manuel: The Power of One Man."[2]

> Jinx did more than just teach kids how to play baseball; he nurtured and shaped fully competent human beings out of the raw materials we were as kids.

> He used the fundamentals of baseball to teach us the fundamentals of life with a grace and kindness few ever come close to mastering.

> I no longer hold the lessons I learned from Jinx like a guidebook imprinted in my head, I behave in accordance with them automatically. In short, I have become Jinx Manuel.

Coaching was Jinx's specialty, but his baseball acumen exposed abilities beyond the game. James was a diligent worker and natural leader. Early in his coaching career, he expended much of his personal effort and some of the money he earned on equipment for the teams. He personally ironed, on each baseball uniform, the patches of the team name. He purchased bats and balls. The expense became a source of conflict with Florine, who wanted every dollar to go toward

---

[2] Jim Sawin, *Urbana Daily Citizen*, June 15, 1987.

family expenses. James innovatively figured out new ways to provide those needs by convincing supporters to contribute financially.

It wasn't only his players who admired him and considered him someone to follow but people of all ages, regardless of race or gender. He was an organizer, often arranging with sponsors of the teams for financing and communicating with the media. He borrowed a cow pasture from a neighbor and constructed a practice facility with a graded and dirt-paved infield and backstop fence. His sons worked with him in maintaining the practice field, but Jinx, usually using borrowed tractors and rigs, did most of the work.

Parents loved how he taught their sons not only baseball skills but also practical lessons and character traits.

He and Florine would put on an annual picnic for the teams at the end of the season. These picnics always were at a major park and included players as well as their families. This was one of the rare events in Springfield that was multiracial, without a hint of the discrimination and division that surrounded other activities. Florine would work all night on huge pans of baked beans and potato salad. Sometimes, Nancy and Frances helped. The event would include games of all types and awards for player accomplishments.

How did they do it? How did they manage to be involved in their community with so many children? Where did Jinx find time to coach teams while working multiple jobs? How did he learn all of the complementary skills of managing sports teams? His intelligence far exceeded his educational level.

In honor of his contributions to Springfield baseball, James was inducted into the Springfield/Clark County Baseball Hall of Fame on January 12, 2008.[3] Coming twenty-one years after his death, the honor was celebrated by Florine and a number of the children, as well as several of the men who, as boys, had been coached by Jinx, along with his long-time friend and fellow inductee, Bill Carter.

---

[3] Jim Sawin, *Urbana Daily Citizen*, January 5, 2008.

9

MATURING FAMILY

(Time period: 1967–1986 and beyond)

The move to Urbana lifted the standard of living for the family. Earned income went up. By that time, James had a steady job at Bauer Brothers Foundry. In addition, he later took on a part-time job as a deputy sheriff. Also, the move made the family healthier and stronger. Farming and raising livestock for food meant bigger and better meals for the growing kids. The associated work meant chores that transformed city-raised children into hardworking country kids. For both the big ones and the little ones, there were new opportunities and challenges that ultimately stimulated their development, enabling them to be physically, mentally, and spiritually stronger; consequently, they were better suited to pursue their places in life.

To the younger Manuel children, their parents were older, compared to the ages that their older siblings had experienced. James and Florine were approaching their fifties. James had retired from coaching boys baseball teams and devoted more of his spare time to raising hogs and working on the small farm. Florine took on part-time work at a school for children with special needs.

Advancement in age did not diminish the parental qualities that were natural for the couple. They were older but also wiser.

The move had the effect of thrusting the younger children into a whole new world. There was space—lots of open, clean, and interesting space for them to play, work, and learn. Like never before, they could run, climb trees, find tadpoles, and pursue new adventures. There was even a playhouse.

James and Florine Manuel in 1982

On the other hand, the move exposed the children to racism that they had not experienced in the predominantly black Harrison Street neighborhood where they had lived in Springfield. Urbana's population had a much lower percentage of African Americans. The school buses were filled with virtually all white kids, except for the Manuel children, and St. Mary School had only one other black family. This change was even more difficult for the older children, who had many friends in Springfield.

When teasing and racial slurs provoked the Manuel children, they fought back. Similar struggles occurred in the lower grades of St. Mary School, where one Manuel child was put back, not because of poor academic performance but because he was "too young"; this child happened to be the only first-grader who could read.

All of the children had new chores to do; some had to rise before dawn. With the hogs and garden, they were now participants in their parents' new enterprise. James called a meeting, in which he asked each of the children what they wanted to do. Michele chose to water the hogs. At first, her chore was routine and rather easy. She ran a hose down to the hog pen and replenished the water daily. But then, winter came. It was too cold to use the hose, but the pigs still needed to be watered. Here is where the parents used the chore to teach. Michele balked at her chore, but James reminded her of what she had volunteered to do and the need to fulfill it, regardless of the difficulty. Consequently, she had to carry buckets of water each day to the hog pen, a much more difficult chore, one that wore calluses on her hands but that also developed her work ethic. The same lesson worked in the garden. One child did not like green beans and didn't want to pick them. When there were no green beans one evening, James sent her to the garden after dark to pick them. What a lesson about responsibility she learned. With little light, scared about what she might encounter, yet facing a father who insisted that she keep her commitment, she worked in the garden that night and never had to do it after dark again.

Playtime changed. As the big ones carried on the practice of playing with and encouraging the development of the little ones, the younger Manuel children experienced less direct contact with their parents than their older siblings had in most types of play, especially baseball. Where Deddy and Mama left off, the big boys and big girls picked up. All of them would play games in the big yard together—baseball, football, volleyball, tag, jump rope, even jacks. It was fun, and later, the little ones reflected on the good that it did for them.

Organized sports interests changed from baseball to the school sports programs, primarily football and track. James was not nearly as involved in these as he had been with baseball. He had coached Charles, Martin, Harry, Greg, Sherman, and Tony. The youngest boys—Michael, Chris, Paul, and Sean—did not experience him as a coach but as a parent who enthusiastically supported them at the farm by virtually turning it into a sports complex. Boys their age from Urbana would join them there to compete in high jump and pole vault. The youngest four, along with Greg, Sherman, and Tony, played sports in Urbana High School's football and track programs. Having inherited the athleticism of their father, they were each competent in their unique ways, amassing various rewards and honors.

Although James did not coach the youngest four boys, he worked with two of them and their sisters Annette and Jeanette in his other strong talent—music. They sang together as a youth group called the Sensations. The older children at home—Sheena, Sherman, Tony, and Michele—sang together too in a church group known as the Gospel Prophets. Although Florine continued in the Catholic faith, she allowed the children to participate in other church settings in Urbana.

As the first few years passed in Urbana, the older children adjusted. Being involved in the school sports programs helped them gain acceptance. Also, they became deeply involved in resisting racial discrimination, even participating in a walkout at the high school. Initially, James and Florine were opposed to their involvement. Florine even threatened that she would come to the school with a switch and use it on them. But both parents softened, and James got the union at Bauer Brothers Foundry to support the demonstrations. In time, the community came to respect the family and the leadership of the Manuel teens, especially Tony for his work to improve racial relations.

In many ways, Urbana was a fun place to grow up.

One of the favorite pastimes of the Manuel children in Urbana was skating. As teenagers, they frequently went together to the skating rink. Nancy would drive from Springfield to bring her children, who were the same ages as some of their uncles and aunts in Urbana, so that they could all go together to the skating rink. Of course, the Manuel kids had to get permission from their parents. This became a routine: first, asking Florine, who would say, "Yes, if it is okay with your father." Then, asking James, not only for permission but also for the car to drive to the rink. At times, he would respond with, "Yes, if your mother says so." Eventually, with lots of "Yes, ma'am" and "Yes, sir," they would proceed and have a blast together.

Nancy's children

Greg

Sherman

Sheena

Tony

Michele

The big ones in Urbana were in high school together in each grade from freshman to senior. In 1969, Greg graduated from Urbana High School, where he had played on the football and track teams. Before the move, he had attended Springfield's public and Catholic schools. The next year, 1970, Sheena graduated. She and Sherman were twins, but girls often advance through school without delay, while boys—no further comment necessary.

Behind by one year, Sherman graduated in 1971. In 1972, Tony graduated. The boys were major contributors to Urbana High School's football and track teams. Sherman was MVP in his senior year. Tony served as Student Council president in his senior year.

In 1973, Michele graduated from Urbana High School. She contributed to the track team, the pep squad, and the drill team. That same year, she was married to Norman Kenny Adams, and they moved to Washington, DC.

Each of these five brought their unique talents and experiences to the fore as they developed. Greg, who had been in the shadow of his older baseball-playing brothers early in life, emerged as the first to play football. All of his younger brothers would follow his lead. With the farm-boy influence on his physical growth and budding strength, he aspired to enter a career in law enforcement.

Sheena and Sherman grew up with the realization that their lives were nearly cut short in infancy as small twins with early illnesses. They survived and grew strong. Until their teens, Sheena was taller than her brother and enjoyed sports. Sherman too liked sports and, early in life, felt called to a life of service to God and humanity.

Tony reacted to the move to Urbana by feeling isolated at first, having left behind friends, but he found a new mission in life in high school, where he became a leader. His manner of learning, instead of academic study, was by absorbing from people around him and situations in which he found himself.

Michele learned her work ethic from James and Florine, but as a child, she was shy and lacked confidence. She credits Kenny Adams for instilling confidence in her to realize her outer and inner beauty and excel in her abilities. As a teen, she shared clothes with Annette and Jeanette each day in school. But as an adult, she dressed well and worked hard in Washington, DC. Consequently, she got promoted in the IRS.

Annette

Jeanette

Michael

Chris

Paul

Sean

The little ones got their turn to fill the Urbana High School grades. In 1976, Annette and Jeanette graduated. Notable contributions were made by Annette as a cheerleader and Jeanette as a class officer each year, including twice as vice president. In 1977, Michael graduated. He had contributed to the football and track teams. In 1979, Chris graduated. He too had contributed to the track squad. In 1984, Paul and Sean graduated. They also contributed significantly to the football and track squads.

The pole vault records for the school were held and broken successively by Michael, then Chris, then Paul. Sean was a great pole-vaulter too, but a serious injury prevented his involvement in the state finals in his senior year.

Annette and Jeanette were both attractive and talented. During their teens, they took different paths, with Annette having to make it as a young single mother and Jeanette struggling with personal crises. Annette, a participant in the TV show *Soul Train*, pursued a career with the Fox TV network. Jeanette, strengthened by a relationship with Jesus Christ, rose above her problems to go on to a life centered in Christian service.

Michael was musically and artistically talented. Receiving a scholarship to Central State University, he developed academically but lacked goals in life, until he moved to California, was encouraged by Frances, and reenrolled in college to finish his degree.

Chris had to fight his way through life. Whether fighting on the bus due to racial taunts from white children or feeling held back by teachers in school, he relied on his image of himself and of the family he was part of as the "smartest and best-looking" among people around him. Muhammad Ali, whose self-confidence and braggadocio never conceded to put-downs, had an impact on his life. He even was told that he and his brothers looked like Ali. He learned early that he could do whatever he wanted to do and succeed.

Paul liked growing up in a big family. Because he was youngest, he was a loner, but Sean's adoption helped. Playing sports with older brothers athletically stimulated him. At the same time, because of dyslexia, he struggled in school, having to learn visually instead of by reading. Chores taught him valuable lessons of work. Paul went on to excel in school football and track. His football record was undefeated from seventh grade through tenth. His junior and senior years had only one loss each, with his senior-year team finishing runner-up in Ohio. In track, he was Ohio pole-vault champion in his senior year, and he still holds the record for his school. He went on to achievements at Mt. San Antonio College in California and Ohio State University.

Thus, the mid-1980s concluded the years of primary and secondary school attendance by Manuel children. The period from the first Manuel child starting school to the last one graduating covered forty years! To many parents, twenty years would seem like plenty. James and Florine are to be commended and congratulated for such an amazing accomplishment. Through it all, they stayed strong and fully supportive of their rapidly growing family. There were, however, anxious moments.

During the early 1970s, Florine suffered what was then termed a mental breakdown without being medically diagnosed. It was brief and did not involve hospitalization. She had encountered a similar episode in late 1943 and through parts of 1944, after the death of her fourth child, Carlotta. Throughout her life, both before and after these incidents, she was mentally sound and physically healthy. The intense stress that she underwent was immeasurable. Only an amazingly strong woman could have carried the weights she bore in pregnancy, parturition, and motherhood.

Through the early seventies and beyond, elsewhere, the Manuel children moved forward in their lives.

In 1970, Charles married Barbara Sims in Las Vegas; their home together was in Los Angeles.

In 1971, Harry married Bonnie Johnson in Los Angeles.

In 1972, Nancy, then divorced from Rendal, married Kenneth Lawson, at which time she and the children moved about a mile away, still on the south side of Springfield.

In 1972, Greg married Valerie Harris in Los Angeles.

In 1973, Michele married Norman K. Adams, nicknamed Kenny, in Urbana and moved to Washington, DC, where both of them worked for the IRS.

In 1974, Greg and Valerie moved back to Springfield, where Greg trained in the Ohio Highway Patrol Academy. Four years later, they moved to Sacramento, California.

In 1975, Tony married Janine Porter in Urbana.

In 1977, Martin and his family relocated to Upstate New York for his job, living in the town of Vestal. In 1979, they relocated to North Carolina for his job, living in Concord, a nearby suburb of Charlotte.

The mid-1970s presented the opportunity for the family to travel. With more and more members relocating to California, James and Florine, along with the children at home, began to visit their loved ones on the West Coast. Travel for a large family without wealth can be humorous, and the Manuel family was no exception. The scene of two adults and five children of the same family traveling on a bus drew attention. So did peanut butter sandwiches and Tang (a powdered juice mixed with water) in rest stops, parks, and, occasionally covertly, in restaurants. The bus trip from Urbana to Los Angeles took more than half a week; the return trip was similar. These scenes were continuous throughout the trip, embarrassing the children. It didn't go on for long, but the stories and laughter continue.

While the family was flexing its collective muscles and stretching its wings, a beloved matriarch was feeling the effects of declining health. Lottie Manuel, suffering from diabetes and the long-term effects of smoking, left her home in Springfield and entered a hospital in Cleveland, near her son Cannellee, for the last time. On September 25, 1972, she died. Her loss was painful. A genuine sweetheart, she was treasured by all the family members, especially her now grown-up grandchildren.

The turn of the decade marked another sad chapter in the family.

In 1981, Charles died of a gunshot wound, a person having fired the gun in self-defense during a home invasion in Los Angeles. For Charles, it was the end of a long struggle involving his mental condition. He had been arrested in 1975 for violent acts, but instead of a prison sentence, he was treated for schizophrenia-paranoia. He was the only one of the seventeen children to be incarcerated. He never recovered from the mental disorder.

To his younger brothers and sisters, he was another one of the big ones. In many ways, he acted out that role—the pioneer of playing sports, holding a job as a teenager, generously sharing gifts at Christmastime, driving a car, and being tough. Most of his siblings recall his boyish mischievousness, and at least one remembers him as the brother who saved his life. All miss him.

Another loss was felt in 1982, when Gus Davis, known to all as Big Daddy, died. He and Big Mama had been loving parents to Florine. He was buried in Ferncliff Cemetery.

The loss of cherished members was painful to everyone in the family, but gaining new family members alleviated some of the sense of loss by the introduction of new personalities, spouses of the now-grown-up children.

In 1981, Jeanette married Fred Carter in Canton, Ohio.

In 1983, Chris married Loretta Butler in Los Angeles.

In 1983, Sherman married Joline Hibbs in Urbana.

In 1984, Michael married Cheryl Barnes in Los Angeles.

In 1988, Annette married Ben Roberts in Los Angeles.

One by one, each of the children grew up, left home, and found jobs during a time of economic expansion and better opportunities for black workers. Greg fulfilled his dream of becoming a law enforcement officer. Sherman began his pursuit of finding ways to serve his fellow humans. Tony started a construction business. Sheena entered cosmetology and later worked in construction. Michele, Annette, and Jeanette started working in administrative jobs and moved up as new opportunities opened to them. Michael became a mechanical engineer in an automobile company. Chris joined the US Army and later moved on to the Army Special Forces in 1990. Paul enlisted in the US Army that same year and was deployed in Kuwait to fight against Iraq in what was known as Desert Storm.

In 1991, Chris married Sabene Stolte in Germany, where the US Army had stationed him.

In 1992, Sean married Erica Wilson in Urbana, where they lived until later moving to Los Angeles.

In 1995, Paul married Beverly Mitchell in Urbana. The couple moved to Chicago Heights, Illinois, and later to San Antonio, Texas.

In 1996, Sheena married Brett Todd Baker in Urbana, where they continue to live.

By the dawn of the twenty-first century, only a small part of the Manuel family still lived in Urbana, and none of the children lived in Springfield. The Manuel family, however, had left a mark on Urbana. Florine was well known and, in some ways, was a virtual celebrity. The disposition of the community toward the family definitely was not that of unwelcome transplants from Springfield—if it ever was. An illustration of the favorable posture that the name Manuel evokes was experienced by one of the spouses, who, while shopping in one of Urbana's large supermarkets, found herself mistakenly at the register without her purse. The store clerk gave her credit because she was a Manuel.

One of the Manuel children who grew up in Urbana said, "We were poor but happy." That short statement sums up that second stage of the family. The same could have been said of the first stage in Springfield. To be poor but happy turns out to be a statement of the character of James and Florine, character that they, in turn, led their children to develop. The family name exemplifies that character and its remarkable strength.

We will look more deeply into the family name and its relationship to character and strength in the last chapter of this book.

10

AUGUST 18, 1987

(Time period: 1980–1987)

Before 1980, James's brothers and sister had never been together in one photo. That changed at a family reunion at the Manuel home in Urbana. Age had crept up on the family. Cornelius, nicknamed Crix, was frail after weight loss caused by cancer. George, Cannellee (Cank), Zeola (Zeke) and James (Jinx) joined him in the photo, their first and last time before a camera together. It was a wonderful reunion. In one year, however, Crix had died, and six months later, Cank died, both of cancer. Zeke and George lived for another fifteen and nineteen years, respectively, but both of them fought cancer before their deaths.

Jinx, Crix, Zeke, Cank, George

James's favorite drink was sweet tea. Florine would prepare a batch in a pan that contained about two gallons. He could drink it all in a few days. The tea was delicious, but the large amount of sugar in it eventually took its toll on James's health.

He was a solidly built man, with a large bone and muscle structure and little fat, so it was immediately noticeable in the early 1980s when he started to lose weight, raising fears of cancer that appeared to run in his family. Frances, who worked at UCLA Hospital, arranged for him to travel to Los Angeles for examination. The diagnosis was type 2 diabetes .

The doctors recommended dietary changes to contain the disease and to reduce the requirement for insulin treatment. Florine worked diligently on his diet plan, preparing more frequent meals and managing his sugar intake. For several years, the meal management worked.

James, then a supervisor at Bauer Brothers Foundry in Springfield, where he had worked for over twenty years, was nearing retirement age. He had planned major changes to the management of the family finances, including paying off the mortgage on their home. Declining health prompted him to consider accelerating his plan.

In early 1987, he began to feel increasing pain in his upper abdomen. Examinations by his doctor were inconclusive. After a month, the pain intensified, causing him to skip his sixty-eighth birthday party. His family, alarmed, made arrangements for him to return to UCLA Hospital for a more expert diagnosis. After exploratory surgery, incurable pancreatic cancer was the diagnosis.

Everyone was shocked! Incurable? One of the children wrote a letter to him while he was still in California, recovering from the surgery. The letter, from which the following excerpt is taken, summarized the family's reaction:

> In one way, your sickness is hard to accept because my view of you has always been one of a small boy looking up at his towering father. Your strength, it seems, should always be there ... You and mom ... almost superhuman ... have affected us and ultimately, the whole world. ... You didn't dump 17 more problems upon humankind. You set an example of giving, and you taught us values that make it possible for us to be assets to the world. If there was a way of evaluating the contribution of two people to the black race in the USA, you and mom would rate at the top along with notable people like Martin Luther King. Your contribution was not a public display but a quiet boost to the one area that black America and the world needs most ... I know that you haven't thought of it that way, and many of us did not while we were too young to appreciate your efforts. But what I am saying here is no exaggeration. Dad, this is just a long way to say that we love you. And we hope that we can copy the wonderful characteristics that make you and mom what you are.

James returned home, paid off the house and car, and sold the hogs. Florine was so stunned that she went about in a daze, not knowing what to do.

When word got around of James's terminal illness, family and friends agreed to express their respect and love by gathering with him on Father's Day.

Many of the men he had coached as boys came, some hundreds of miles, for the occasion. Over three hundred people spent the day in the front yard of the Manuel home in Urbana. For many, it was a wonderful reunion, but most of all, it honored one who was, in effect, a father to hundreds.

Nancy and Larry moved in to help prepare meals and provide care for James as he grew weaker. Pain was constant. In spite of his difficulties, he remained proud. He insisted on driving to shop for groceries. A smoker most of his adult life, he had given it up until late, when he sought a little enjoyment in the midst of his pain, knowing that it was too late to quit. Always striving to be strong, he remained independent until last day.

When the cancer spread to his lungs, it ended quickly, with one day in the hospital. The fluid in his lungs spared him any further suffering. The dear husband of Florine and father of their children breathed his last on August 18, 1987.

He was buried in Ferncliff Cemetery in Springfield.

The mark that this man's life left on the world will forever be seen as a mark of beauty, nobility, and strength in the people he humbly served and, most of all, in his posterity.

11

FAMILY AGAIN

(Time period: 1988–2009)

After James's death, the family went through a period of adjustment, as together they sought to cope with his absence. Overall, he had been the unquestioned and unchallenged leader, except for those times when Florine made her disagreement known. He and Florine, like all married couples, had their disagreements, sometimes obvious to all of the children, now and then boiling over into arguments, even vehement on occasion. They always reconciled, however, and proceeded together. Actually, they functioned with specific roles, in which the leadership might alternate from one to another, with the support role belonging to the one not in the lead. But most of the time, in their partnership, James was the leader and Florine the support.

Florine's motherly role was always strong, and she was the primary cook, clothing provider, and homemaker. Also, she led the family in religious matters. With James no longer there, she tried to fill the leadership gap but was not always adept in doing so. Family harmony, with each of the children willingly supporting the parents and peacefully coexisting with each other, had been the family's basic mode of operation—allowing, of course, for individual clashes and areas of differences. With James's strong leadership no longer there, new conflicts arose.

The first conflict revolved around the Middle Urbana Road property and who would assume the lead and ownership. At the time of James's death, Nancy and her husband, Larry Hicks, were living there to care for him. Of course, Florine lived there too, although for several months after James's death, she was away, visiting her children. She had benefited from Nancy and Larry's living in the home, and she was content for them to remain there and assume it as their residence, which they did for a while. However, she did not express to the rest of the family any long-term intentions for the property, and nothing was documented. Not wanting to disappoint others who were interested in having it, she left the resolution uncertain. This uncertainty and the suspicions and disputes that developed went on for several years.

Florine could not maintain the property, and for much of the time, because she traveled around the country, spending time with her children on both coasts, even visiting Hawaii, she was not there.

In the meantime, a new farm property—seventy-eight acres; a mix of pasture, cultivated cropland, woods, a pond, barns, a large main house, and a second house—became the source of investment interest for several members of the family. They formed a corporation and bought the property, arranging for Florine to move to the main house on the property. She loved her beautiful, spacious new home, and it immediately became the center of all family activities, such as reunions and other occasional get-togethers, including two weddings.

Through negotiation and with the arbitration of one of the family members, the Middle Urbana Road property became Sheena's home. Soon afterward, she arranged to sell a small subdivided parcel to Nancy and her husband, Larry, to build a house on it.

All the while, dissension about the two properties led to hard feelings and conflicts previously not experienced. At that time, one of the family members composed a song titled "Family Again" and brought a band and singing group to the new home for a gathering for all to consider the toll of disharmony. Below are the lyrics of the song:

Family Again

Remember the times together
Surviving stormy weather?
Times were always so rough
Getting by was so tough.

Remember the way it used to be
When all we had was family?
Never having a doubt
Things would someday work out.

If we rally around each other
And take care of fathers and mothers,
Then together we stand, we'll walk hand in hand
And be family again.

Are we about to lose the race?
Prosperity took love's place.
Caring turned into hate,
But it's never too late.

If we rally around each other
And take care of sisters and brothers,
Then together we stand, we'll walk hand in hand
And be family again.

Children need a home
To never live alone
All of us must care for our own.

Open up your heart
Make a brand-new start
We can find a way, a way.

If we rally around each other
And take care of fathers and mothers,
Then together we stand, we'll walk hand in hand
And be family again.

If we rally around each other
And take care of sisters and brothers,
Then together we stand, we'll walk hand in hand
And be family again.

Let's be family again, let's be family again
When we're family again:
No more homeless people
No drugs or crime in the streets
No abandoned children
We're all in harmony
When we're family again, when we're family again
The whole world will be a better place,
When we're family again!

©1994 Martin Manuel

Reconciliation was not immediate, but in the years that followed, the tensions lessoned, and harmony returned.

Florine was a big reason for the restoration. Everyone wanted to rally around her, and she, with her exuberant personality, always made it easy and fun. Frequently, she traveled to spend time with family members—her children and their families. Special times, such as Christmas, Thanksgiving, and the Fourth of July, were traditional gathering times for the family. Everyone would come to her home, first on Middle Urbana Road and later on the new seventy-eight-acre farm property.

For her seventy-fifth birthday, her children planned a big surprise. First, one of the daughters who lived in California came a week before the birthday to stay with her. Next, they attached a huge banner with the words "Happy 75th Birthday" to the side of the barn that faced US 36. Drivers on the highway honked when they saw the banner. But the big surprise took place in what was to become her new home, which was under renovation. This home was the other house on the property, about fifty feet from the main house.

While she was living in the main house, she could see the renovation underway simply by looking out her kitchen window and observing about a dozen workers in and around the house. One of the Manuel sons in the construction business was overseeing the remodeling project. His renovation crew was actually his brothers and sisters. Each of them wore hoodies that masked their true identities. This went on for about a week.

On her birthday, the daughter staying with her said, "Mom, let's go over to see how the remodeling is going." She and Florine walked to the door and opened it to see, to her surprise, one of the Manuel daughters in a hoodie. Florine shouted, "Oh!" and hugged her, only to be touched on the shoulder by another in a pulled-down hoodie. Again, she shouted, "Oh!" One by one, each of her children pulled off their hoodies and all shouted, "Happy birthday!" The party started, and Florine was ecstatic at her special birthday surprise of most of her children back home, just like the old days, with her.

The next summer, the new property was host to the wedding of one of the sons and his bride.

The following year, there was a family reunion on the farm, and the wedding ceremony of one of the daughters took place in the front yard. The reunion went on for most of the week, with nearly every family member participating.

Three years afterward, there was another reunion and celebration of Florine's eightieth birthday. This started the tradition of a reunion and birthday celebration every other year through her eighty-eighth.

When she turned ninety, two hundred family members and friends came together in a rented facility in Urbana, with a large reception area, auditorium, and banquet hall for the celebration. The event, with interviews, was featured on WRGT-TV in Dayton.

The reunion started a week before her birthday, and the party went on for two more days.

These joyous events, centered on this well-beloved mother, brought about the restoration of the family harmony of the past, and that harmony continues.

All of her sixteen living children came to celebrate her ninetieth birthday. Pictured above, all standing around their seated mother, are (left to right) Jeanette, Martin, Frances, Paul, Sherman, Michael, Tony, Sean, Chris, Nancy, Greg, Annette, Sheena, Drucilla, Michele, and Harry.

In addition to Florine's ninetieth birthday celebration, a portion of the seventy-eight-acre farm was adorned with mementos of James and Florine's legacy through their children. The property included an area of old trees, primarily oak and quite large.

Florine was shown this area that one compared to a savannah. Each of seventeen trees was labeled with the name of one of the children, and a large apple tree near the entrance had an attached plaque that read, "Welcome to the Manuel Family Tree Forest," with the names of the children encircling a photo of the parents.

Below this, the plaque has the following words printed on a brass plate:

> This apple tree is symbolic of bearing fruit (and) is dedicated to Florine and James Manuel. The Bible reads in Genesis 9–1 to be fruitful and increase in number and fill the Earth (paraphrased). Mom and Daddy complied with the word and had 17 children. We the children of James and Florine Manuel thank (them) for a job well done.

The family would have more than twenty years to regain the stability that came with their anchor, James. And they did, largely because of their sail, Florine. That stability remains.

12

A SPECIAL MEETING

(Time period: 2010)

The election of Barack Obama as the forty-fourth president of the United States in 2008 was thrilling to Florine and her family. To an eighty-nine-year-old African American woman, who had struggled all her life with adversity, solely because of her African heritage, it was inconceivable to her that a family of African heritage could become occupants of the White House. Even more, she never dreamed of meeting President Obama.

For months after her ninetieth birthday, Florine had felt the effects of a decline in her health. Increasingly, she spent long hours in her recliner in front of the TV set during the day and went to bed early at night. She had round-the-clock in-home nursing care, all meals prepared for her, and one of her children living in to keep her company and take care of other needs.

Around midyear, she heard that two of her sons were to meet with the president, his staff, and political representatives from Ohio, invited by Governor Ted Strickland, to present their contributions to the 2003 Iraq war and the reconstruction of Iraq that followed.

"I want to be there," she said. Family members cautioned her about her condition, the toll that travel and attendance would take, and the unlikelihood that the president would have time for any personal meetings.

But Florine, undeterred, insisted that she would be strong enough to attend and that she would only be there as an observer. She won. The morning of the meeting, Florine rallied her strength, prepared herself, and dressed like a queen. A third son escorted her, providing a wheelchair to limit her walking and give her comfortable seating. A daughter-in-law, wife of one of the attending sons, accompanied them.

The president spoke to the large gathering and, afterward, noticed Florine sitting near the front in her wheelchair. Mr. Obama walked away from the lectern toward Florine and greeted her.

When she mentioned to the president that she was there with several of her sixteen living children, he expressed interest in knowing more and issued a directive to one of his staff members to follow up. The follow-up did not occur, but photos taken by the White House photographer and shared with the family visually capture the memorable moment that the three sons, a daughter-in-law, and Florine had with America's first black president.

The *Urbana Daily Citizen* ran an article[4] about the meeting,

---

[4] Kathleen Fox, *Urbana Daily Citizen*, September 21, 2010.

including a photo (not shown) of daughter-in-law Dawn Manuel; her husband, Tony Manuel; President Barack Obama; Florine; Chris Manuel; and Sherman Manuel, standing side by side.

The humorous outcome of the meeting was that because the president spent so much time talking with Florine, there was no time left for the planned meetings with others, including her sons. Neither of them expressed disappointment, realizing that the more important meeting involved America's first black president and a special ninety-year-old black mother.

13

July 3, 2011

(Time period: 1987–2011)

Florine at 90

By her looks, Florine seemed to never age.

Even at eighty, she looked like a fiftysomething woman, and she acted even younger. After James's death, she shifted into a new phase of her life—traveling, from North Carolina to California and wherever her children settled.

In 1992, she moved from the Middle Urbana Road home into

the main house on the seventy-eight-acre farm, purchased jointly by several of her children. The property, mostly farmland along US 36, about one-half mile east of Urbana, was envisioned as investment land, but first, it served as her home for the next ten years.

With the children grown, Florine and Drucilla lived together while the property was developed with the addition of a home in a remodeled structure. After it was finished, it became their home while the main house was rented out, mostly to extended family members.

Throughout her years with James, she dwelt as his partner and lover but in the shadow of his local notoriety, in light of his success in baseball and especially coaching. She was the figurative wind beneath his wings, always there supporting him but also his inspiration. Her personality—gregarious, funny, and extroverted—sometimes clashed with his quiet, reserved, playful-but-serious persona. "Flo," as he called her, liked to clown around, as he would say. One of her children secretly labeled her "Clown Manuel," telling her that secret when she was ninety and, as expected, getting a hearty laugh from her.

Starting at her seventy-fifth, her children celebrated her birthday every other year with increasing intensity. Like an extended party, Florine thoroughly enjoyed these wonderful times with her family. She danced joyously, even when, later, she used a walker to help her get around.

In her eighties, she had knee replacement surgery for both knees and recovered quickly, standing more than an inch taller with her newly straightened legs.

Her friends marveled as she enjoyed her life, and they wondered where she had found the fountain of youth. But her body internally was not as young as she looked. She suffered from kidney problems in her mid-thirties, and the birth of each child seemed to weaken them. Medical treatment throughout her eighties helped, but renal failure finally set in after she turned ninety.

By then, she was living in a modern duplex apartment in the heart of Urbana. She had moved from the farmhouse in 2002 into a senior center for several years and, from there, back to Middle Urbana Road in a newer house that had been added to the property. Her children made all of these arrangements as they sought the best living conditions for her. In the apartment, at times, one of the children would live in the spare bedroom to be there to look out for her. To assist her with meals and medical needs, her children arranged live-in nursing care.

While there, her ninetieth birthday was celebrated by over two hundred people in a large rented facility with a dining hall and stage for performances. Part of the celebration was featured on a TV station in Dayton. All of her children participated.

The next year, her health further declined, but she got a lift when she met with President Barack Obama, as mentioned in detail in the previous chapter.

In late 2010, while she was receiving regular dialysis, she suffered from an infection and several months later was diagnosed with colon cancer. Florine elected not to have surgery.

On July 3, 2011, Florine died, with her children around her.

She had lived a modest life, but she was celebrated as a queen. It was her stated intention, even when she was in her forties, that she wanted an elaborate funeral. Her children did their best to ensure that the closing years of her life were enjoyable. She had borne all of them, and they recognized that she deserved the best.

The same was true of her funeral, her celebration of life. A bishop, who was her great-nephew, and two pastors presided, her former and current, who was a priest at St. Mary Catholic Church, the church she returned to in her last few years. Her casket was carried from the church building to the cemetery in a horse-drawn carriage.

She was buried in Oak Dale Cemetery in Urbana.

Her children, fully mature adults, mourned her death but, even more, celebrated her life with all of the wonderful fruit, memories, and laughter it brought.

14

MANUEL CHILDREN TODAY

(Time period: 2012–2020)

After Florine's death, the family entered a new phase, without the parents who had given it the rock-solid foundation and zest for life it had enjoyed. However, because of the strength of the family, exhibited in each of the first-generation children, the family remained close-knit and continued moving forward. Several now have reached retirement age and are active in new ways. Most have continued in their career activities.

———————— ❖ ————————

Nancy worked as a registered nurse (RN) after graduating from Sinclair Community College in Dayton. She had dreamed of being a nurse when in high school and had applied to a class to become a certified nursing assistant (CNA), but there were no openings. She noticed that some of her white fellow students got into the class, and she became discouraged and decided to quit school and get married. Her desire to work in nursing did not go away, and when her daughter, Shari, enrolled in Sinclair Community College to pursue her nursing degree over twenty years later, Nancy decided to enroll too. The two, mother and daughter, attended together, graduated together, and became nurses together. While working as a nurse at Champaign Nursing Home, Nancy continued her training, achieving an associate's degree. Later, she worked as supervisor of nurses at Alterra Sterling House, where she again met some of her former fellow high school CNA graduates, this time as their supervisor. She went on from there to work as an RN at Hartland of Urbana, Springfield Community Hospital, and Mercy Hospital in Springfield, before putting her career on hold for health reasons.

Frances aspired to attend medical school and dreamed of visiting and living in exotic places. Disappointed that her maternal grandmother's stated intent to put her through medical school did not come to pass and lacking the means to afford entry otherwise, she went to work part-time and trained in a doctor's office in Springfield after she graduated from high school. A few years later, she moved to Los Angeles, where she worked as a nursing assistant. Next, she became a certified x-ray technician and medical office administrator, using her expert administration skills at Daniel Freeman Hospital and UCLA Hospital, both in Los Angeles. After retiring from UCLA Hospital, she moved to Las Vegas, Nevada, and started a second career, working in the medical field there, as well as applying her administration skills to a new area in insurance with Sierra Health Services, where she contributed to various roles until her retirement in 2009.

Frances struggled with five bouts of cancer, undergoing treatment over the fifteen years. In 2019, she was once again diagnosed with lung cancer. This time, to preserve the best quality of life, she decided to forego chemotherapy. In July 2020, she fought the disease into its spread to her brain. After successful removal of an aggressive malignant tumor in Las Vegas, she was moved to therapy, where she contracted COVID-19 and died. Her siblings and family watched this fighter take on each round with determination and cheerfulness.

Through it all, she never complained and always maintained that infectious smile.

This is her—always looking like a beauty queen. She pioneered the move to the West Coast and helped many brothers and sisters to follow. She is sorely missed.

Martin loved science and technology and dreamed of being a scientist. As he and other family members watched a football game on TV and a commercial came on for Georgia Tech University, he looked at James and said, "That's where I want to go to college." James's eyes slowly turned toward him, and his answer told Martin that his father did not approve. It was not Martin's first experience with disapproval, and many more were to come throughout his life. However, he did not then realize that his parents would spearhead his post-high school education by gifting him with enrollment in a tech school, which opened opportunity for him in the data processing and computer fields. He was hired by the IBM Corporation to work in Chicago as a customer engineer and, briefly, as an instructor in the IBM Education Center. At LaSalle Extension University, he studied business management to broaden his skills. IBM transferred him, first to New York State, where he worked as a technical writer, and from there to Charlotte, North Carolina, again as a technical writer and manager. He went on to be a senior manager in IBM Charlotte before retiring from a career rife with racially discriminatory resistance but rich in experience.

Afterward, he started a second career in Charlotte as a church pastor, serving congregations for over ten years and writing a book, before taking leave from pastoral ministry to move to Redmond, Washington, during the health crisis of a family member there. Two years later, after returning to Charlotte, he resumed service in pastoral ministry, completed his master's in pastoral ministry from Grace Communion Seminary, and published two more books. He continues today as a writer of web magazine articles and books.

Harry served as a US Marine in the Vietnam War. While there, he told an officer over him (a lieutenant) that his tactics of general warfare would not work in jungle warfare, but his advice was dismissed. Instead, the lieutenant reassigned him, and he was deployed to the most hazardous place, the DMZ. He, unlike the lieutenant, survived. After he left Vietnam, he was trained on the Redeye missile and proved he was capable of shooting down warplanes.

After three years in the Marine Corps, he returned a veteran, ready to pursue his plans. He attended college in Los Angeles, taking classes in business and accounting, while working for Thrifty Drugstore. Thrifty had openings for management trainees. Although his interest was in accounting, he took the job, but instead of management training, he was assigned to the ice cream department and challenged to close a store, a task he had not been trained to do. To the surprise of his "trainer," he met the challenge. Later, a highly touted corporate adviser said to him, "With your personality, you will never be a manager." Harry was not intimidated; in time, he became a store manager, and later, when he became a district manager, he became that adviser's boss. He went on from there to become assistant vice president. After he had been there twenty years Thrifty was bought out by Rite Aid. Harry left but went on to manage other stores, including Toys "R" Us, Best Buy, HomeBase, Kmart, and Marshalls.

During his career at Thrifty, Harry followed his father, James, by coaching Little League Baseball for eight years, working with economically deprived boys in a poor-performing league. He became league president, and turned it around. Now retired, he and his family continue to live in Southern California.

———— •·•·• ————

Drucilla, or Dru, as some called her, was a well-beloved child of James and Florine and cherished sister of her siblings. She endured a disability all of her life, but it did not stop her from completing her education and pursuing her dream as a gifted artist. In 2010, she had the honor of having her self-portrait exhibited at the Smithsonian American Art Museum/National Portrait Gallery in Washington, DC.

In 2012, she was diagnosed with ovarian cancer.

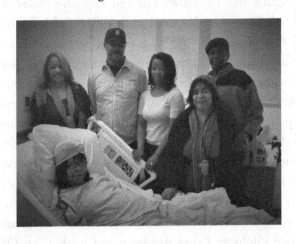

Above: In recovery, with Frances, Greg, Jeanette, Nancy, and Sheena, at Ohio State University Hospital

Left: Before surgery, an affectionate moment with Jerome

She is missed by all.

In early 2013, she had successful surgery at Ohio State University Hospital. On the day she was to be discharged after recovery, she suffered a fatal heart attack. Years prior, she had undergone heart bypass surgery.

Greg moved to Los Angeles after finishing high school and attended several colleges. His interest in law enforcement came from watching the TV shows *FBI* and *Highway Patrol*. While in high school, he expressed interest in the FBI, but his football coach asserted that he would never be accepted because of his race. An incident involving his dad sparked his interest in the highway patrol. He had witnessed his father jailed for driving with a burned-out headlight and not having the cash to pay the fine. Greg envisioned being a policeman whose service would include compassion.

His first opportunity came with the Los Angeles Police Department, but he decided to pass on it because of a deep dislike of the racism he saw in the department, which had repeatedly pulled him over while he was driving, at times with guns drawn, when there was no violation involved. He moved to Ohio to attend the Ohio State Highway Patrol Academy and work as an Ohio state highway patrol officer. After four years, he and his family moved back to California, where he joined the California Highway Patrol (CHP), stationed in Sacramento. Over the years, he had seventeen different assignments there, from officer to assistant chief. For six months, he served as acting chief. Part of his training and experience included attendance in the FBI National Academy. Greg valued the training but already had chosen the highway patrol over the FBI. As a law enforcement officer, he knew how to manage situations with offenders without always resorting to force. Now retired from the CHP, he continues to live in California.

Sheena has a gift that makes her a natural designer, builder, and craftsperson. She discovered this gift when she was in her thirties. Without in-class or on-the-job training, she can visualize, with one look, the outcome of a construction project. Florine kidded her that she was a builder in a former life. Before she discovered this gift, she had moved to Los Angeles. Needing work, she studied cosmetology in a nearby beauty school and opened a salon. After a scary incident that threatened the life of one of her young children, she decided to return to Urbana.

After she got settled, she was looking for a job and, at the suggestion of her brother, started working with David Clark, who had a painting business. She has worked with him off and on for seventeen years. In between, she worked in the Urbana Youth Center with children with behavioral problems. She also taught construction at Urban Youth Academy in Springfield. After a fire in her home, the Middle Urbana Road house where she had grown up, she completely redesigned and remodeled the interior. She reflected on something that she had been told when she purchased that house without acceptable credit; the banker told her that he had approved the loan request because "you are the hardest working woman I have ever known." She also reflects on the undeserved blessings she has received, explainable only as the grace of God.

Twice, she has fought leukemia and has survived. Today, she still works on various construction projects.

———————————

Sherman learned a song when he was a fourth-grade student at St. Mary School about Zacchaeus, a man mentioned in the Gospel of Luke as one Jesus especially liked. Sherman wondered why Jesus liked him more than others and learned that it was about his humility and willingness to give and serve. That lesson stuck with him and helped to channel his life.

After a short stay in Los Angeles, Sherman returned to Urbana to set up a community assistance center to house public service agencies. He served as a youth director and youth program coordinator. When he was in his mid-twenties, he purchased a building in downtown Urbana for the center, which became the location of many organizations that serve the Urbana community.

Later, he worked as a manager at the Honda assembly plant. While there, he developed an innovative method of seat-belt installation, which resulted in a trip to Japan, followed by implementation in Honda plants around the world. Because Honda had discriminated against him when he first sought to be hired, a court judgment awarded him a payout and pension.

Another of his community contributions was Climbers Mountain, a family entertainment center with a miniature golf course in Urbana.

———————————

Tony has worked in the construction industry for over forty-five years as a licensed carpenter, a licensed general contractor, a 1&2 family dwelling inspector, and rehabilitation adviser. He has participated in numerous legal proceedings as a construction subject-matter expert. He was an early adopter of the use of insulated concrete forms (ICF) in home construction. He taught building code classes at Clark State College and civil engineering at Sinclair College in Dayton.

Tony got involved in the defense industry during the wars in Afghanistan and Iraq, starting STAN Solutions, a company that offered advanced technological products and personnel on the ground for postwar support of US military forces and projects of allied government for law enforcement and reconstruction. Tony and his brother Chris were presented a certificate of appreciation from the United States Army Intelligence and Security Command for their work and support of Operation Iraqi Freedom.

Since the withdrawal of large numbers of American ground forces, Tony has worked on the use of similar cutting-edge technologies and processes in peaceful applications. He continues to live in Dayton, Ohio, and uses his skills in engineering and construction projects.

Michele launched her career with the IRS shortly after she married Kenny Adams, who was already working for the IRS. She started working in a group of about forty women, and she quickly distinguished herself by her excellence in her work; she worked hard and always was professional in her appearance and speech. Michele and Kenny together had assignments in the IRS that started in Washington, DC, and led them from there to Chicago, St. Louis, South Dakota, and Atlanta.

Shortly after the move to Atlanta, Kenny, the love of her life, battled with cancer and died. Michele went on working there until she retired. After retirement, she moved back to Urbana, where, besides her role as grandmother, she has worked with her new husband in his auto shop.

Annette moved to Los Angeles when she was twenty, hoping to become an actress; soon after, she was invited to be a dance participant on the *Soul Train* TV show. After earning an accounting certification from a community college, she was hired into the accounting department of Metromedia, which later became Fox TV. After developing computer skills in the Billing and Payroll Departments and teaching herself to operate a teleprompter, she was assigned to work with new programs and lead other staff members. Next, she became a tape operator and started working with an editor as second assistant, quickly mastering the technology. Assigned to the overnight shift to make dubs, she devised a computerized system that saved dubbing time, opening the opportunity for her to be second engineer on the morning shift. There, by watching the editor, she learned to edit and, in time, won over clients in a male-dominated task. Broadcast Operations invited her to work on their side as technical director in live broadcasting, accommodating her need for time with children. She transitioned to an automated system of rolling tape and was asked to train other people in the company; subsequently, she was engineer in charge. When Fox wanted to expand, she was asked to start Fox Cable and oversee two hundred employees. She developed a training system that everyone who worked for network or cable went through. She was offered a director job at a problem area, Fox Sports International, and was placed in charge of building it and was promoted to executive director. After the merger of Fox and Disney made her job redundant, she retired after thirty-nine years at Fox. Currently, she serves as chairwoman for Hope of the Valley, a rescue mission with which she became involved as a volunteer through the Life Group of her church. In this new role, she leads a team of community leaders.

Jeanette dreamed of working in the airline industry after graduation from high school. She attended a tech school in Coral

Gables, Florida, to obtain a degree that would prepare her to be a flight attendant. The school promised job placement opportunities, but she noticed that none of the black students got jobs, while most or all of the white students did. Instead of a job lead, the associate school director repeatedly asked her to become a nanny for his kids. She left there and moved to California, where she hoped to work as a flight attendant. There too she was unable to find a job.

While there, the Holy Spirit spoke to her to return to Ohio. There, she met and married her husband and started to build a family. She worked as a supervisor with Nationwide Insurance and later Blue Cross and Blue Shield Insurance, where she received a buyout. The same day, her husband got promoted to move to Columbus. While raising her three children, she did in-home art shows and later worked part time with Abbott Labs, receiving full benefits. Her passion in church work is children's ministry, where she served until she later became manager of women's workout facility. Afterward, she worked in administration for the church. Also, she and her husband serve as marriage mentors. Most recently, she was hired at McDonald's GBS Finance. She is close to finishing her bachelor's degree in organizational leadership at Otterbein University.

Michael was always fascinated with learning about cars and was interested in building and fixing things. After chores, he could always be found building clubhouses and go-carts and designing something. He attended St. Mary Catholic School and experienced racism but learned how to use it as motivation and excel in sports. He also received a scholarship and attended Central State University as an art major. From there, he took drafting at Clark State College. He moved to California in 1981 and began doing drafting and writing NC (numerical control) computer programs to produce sheet-metal amplifiers. He moved from that position to become a senior engineer at Honda R&D North American and received his bachelor of science degree in mechanical engineering while working at Honda. There, he set up the facility that produced the Honda Accord Wagon and developed a new process for prototyping cars.

He went on a mission trip to South Africa, where his life changed forever, as he discovered his purpose while in Africa.

He won a lawsuit against Honda, relocated to Ohio, and started DOIT training and development. His engineering background equipped him with skills to lead by example.

He got a house for one dollar in historical Wright-Dunbar Village and began renovating properties while training people from the community. The vision he was blessed with in Africa was piloted in Dayton. He started a ninth- through twelfth-grade charter school in 2004. He continued working with youth and Africans in Dayton while doing training. He was selected as Mentor of the Year in 2017. He became an ordained elder and a teacher at Dayton Public Schools, where he continues operating in his purpose. DOIT currently offers the BEE Process (Building Economic Empowerment) for adults and junior engineer programs for youth.

Chris made a career of being a soldier in the US Army. After his initial enlistment, he reenlisted into the Army Special Forces Green Berets, with the goal of becoming a chief warrant officer (CWO). Through his education and assignments, he learned to speak three languages. The US State Department made use of his skills and services in demining several countries. Also, he served in many African countries, Kuwait, Bosnia, and Afghanistan after the US declared war in response to the 9/11 attacks. His technological achievements with unmanned aerial vehicles (UAV) gained him lead roles in the development of new technologies and opened the door for him to receive more formal excellent training and education opportunities. Consequently, in 2004, he was the first army warrant officer to graduate from the Naval Postgraduate School, achieving a master's degree.

After leaving active duty, he worked for the Sierra Nevada Corporation (SNC) as a corporate vice president. He continued his service in the Army Reserve at the Army Cyber Institute as a research fellow at West Point. He is currently the Associate Dean of Research at the Naval Postgraduate School in California, where he and his family continue to live. He also serves as the Naval Postgraduate School's director of both the Emerging Technologies Consortium and the Central Coast Tech Bridge.

Paul enlisted in the US Army shortly before Iraq invaded Kuwait, triggering the Gulf War. He served as a soldier in Kuwait, participating in the ground war labeled Desert Storm. After returning to his base in Texas and being joyously received by Florine, he embarked on his career. After attending Consumer Electronic Training Center in Chicago, he used his electronics training to work as a technical support representative in Chicago for Walgreen's Management Information Systems (WMIS), a contracting company that took over the computing services of WMIS and other companies. He has worked in this field since 1993. In 2017, he moved to San Antonio and now works for the US Department of Defense, doing information technology (IT) remote support for the US military by offering general technical assistance, including accessing their computers and connecting and downloading fixes and upgrades.

Together, Health Issues, Youthful

The year after Florine's death, 2012, the family had its biggest reunion since Florine's ninetieth birthday. All of the family members met in Urbana for the joyous event, except for Martin, who was in Washington State, attending to an ill family member.

In 2015, some sixty-five members of the family gathered for a reunion in Concord, North Carolina. Primarily for health reasons, several of the family members did not attend, but it was a joyous and unifying event.

In 2020, another major reunion was planned, but it was canceled because of the pandemic. Instead, the family members participated in numerous Zoom meetings that served to keep up their communications and relationships. Every living member, as well as a number of their children and grandchildren, participated in these sessions.

Cancer and back problems seemed to plague the family, even in the generation of James and Florine. As of this writing, six of the Manuel children have been diagnosed with some form of cancer. Four continue to survive. Three have been treated for serious degeneration of the spine and back because of injuries earlier in life. They too are survivors.

Although these genetic weaknesses seem to affect most family members, a strong genetic advantage, especially evident in Florine, was passed on to all of her children. That advantage is an extraordinarily youthful appearance. The photo of Frances, a few pages back, was taken when she was seventy. And consider Jeanette's experience: When her daughter Erica was sixteen and Jeanette was forty-six, she went to her daughter's high school to sign for her to go on a school trip. A crowd of students was in the hall, prompting a teacher to tell them to move on to their next classes. The kids took off, and Jeanette stood in line with the other parents. The teacher came into the office, looked at Jeanette, raised his voice, and said, "I told you to go to your class!" All of the adults stared at Jeanette. Erica's cheerleading coach came around the corner as the teacher again shouted, "I said get to class!"

By then, several teachers and administrative staff looked on, and one asked, "Mr. Dale, who are you talking to?"

He answered, "I'm talking to her!"

The cheerleading coach said, "She's not a student. She's Erica and Evan's mother!"

Consider these facts and the statement they make about the Manuel family: There were seventeen biological children and one adopted child; all but four are alive today (as of fall 2020). One was arrested; none was convicted of a felony. The overall contribution to society is beyond calculation. In summary, of the thirteen alive today of the seventeen, there are:

- Two retired nurses
- One celebrated artist
- One retired church pastor and corporate manager
- One retired chain-store executive and Vietnam War veteran
- One retired assistant chief of the California Highway Patrol
- One former owner of a midsized business that served in the rebuilding of Iraq after the 2003 invasion
- One current owner of a nonprofit business that serves educational needs of urban youth
- A mechanical engineer and current school teacher
- Several currently employed in labor or administrative jobs
- One retired TV network executive
- A Gulf War veteran
- A former Army Special Forces Chief Warrant Officer, currently an associate dean of the Naval Postgraduate School

Like their extraordinary parents, the Manuel children have lived as model citizens and contributed significantly to the welfare of their respective communities, as well as the nation.

Although ordinary people, neither these nor their parents conform to any stereotypes: ancient or contemporary, social status, cultural or racial.

All of them shared the common strength that was gained by having to walk uphill in every endeavor. As James had told them, "To be considered equal, you must be better." As he had modeled to them, "Never start a fight, but when attacked, defend yourself and win." He poetically wrote on paper what he mastered in life: "Always do your best." Annette added, "If I could be a fifteen-year-old single mother and become an executive with Fox, anybody can."

15

GRANDCHILDREN AND MORE

(Time period: 1956–2020)

Previously mentioned were the births of Nancy's first four children: Shari, Katonyia, Adriene, and Tyrin, born between 1956 and 1959.

Nancy next gave birth to Rendal Richard, nicknamed Richie, in 1963. The Bass family remained in Springfield, living in several different houses near the Manuel home on Fremont Avenue; they later purchased and lived in that Fremont Avenue home.

In the meantime, Frances gave birth to Tracey Renee in 1965. She grew up with her mother in Los Angeles.

The following year, Sean was born to Charles, and, as previously mentioned, James and Florine later adopted him. Sean grew up with his adopted parents in Urbana, Ohio.

In 1968, Charles's second son, Charles Snodgrass, was born and grew up with his mother in Springfield.

Photo not Available

In 1969, Martin's wife, Genneen, gave birth to their first child, Janet Elliotta, in Harvey, Illinois.

In 1971, Harry's wife, Bonnie, gave birth to Marcus Terrelle in Los Angeles. The family continued to live in Los Angeles.

In 1971, Martin's wife, Genneen, gave birth to Michael Ted Manuel in Harvey, Illinois, a suburb of Chicago. The family moved that year to Maywood, another Chicago suburb.

In 1972, Greg's wife, Valerie, gave birth to Reneisha Nikole. The family continued to live in Los Angeles.

In 1973, Bonnie gave birth to Taneia De'Trese in Los Angeles. The family continued to live there until they moved to Pomona, a suburb of Los Angeles.

In 1973, Theresa gave birth to Latosha Montrell in Urbana. They lived in Urbana until they moved to Los Angeles.

In May 1973, Michael Ted, son of Martin and Genneen, died in Maywood, Illinois. Teddy, as he was nicknamed, was a delightful baby and toddler. He had been born with Down syndrome and a defective heart. He lived to be twenty months old.

In 1974, Michele gave birth to Janine Annette in Washington, DC. The family lived there and afterward relocated to a suburb of Chicago.

In 1974, Martin's wife, Genneen, gave birth to Doreen Jeanette in Maywood, Illinois.

That same year, Charles's third son, Shad, was born in Los Angeles. There, he grew up with his mother and her family.

Photo not Available

In 1974, Tony's wife, Janine, gave birth to James Anthony Jr.

In 1975, Sheena gave birth to Richelle Eloyce in Urbana. They continued to live in Urbana.

In 1975, the first great-grandchild was born when Tyrin, Nancy's daughter, gave birth to Kent Terrell in Springfield.

In 1975, Tony's wife,
Janine, gave birth
to Aaron Dion.
The family lived in
Springfield.

In 1977, Tony's wife,
Janine, gave birth
to Andrew Darion
in Springfield,
having purchased
the Fremont Avenue
home. They remained
there until they later
moved to Urbana.

In 1977, Katonyia,
Nancy's daughter,
gave birth to Eric
Lamonte, the second
great-grandchild, in
Springfield.

In 1978, Shari,
Nancy's daughter,
married Darwin
Mabra in Springfield.

In 1979, Katonyia,
Nancy's daughter,
gave birth to the third
great-grandchild,
Michael Stephen, in
Springfield.

In 1979, Sherman's
wife, Joline, gave
birth to Sheree Nicole
in Urbana.

In 1979, Greg's wife,
Valerie, gave birth to
Scott Christopher in
Los Angeles.

In 1980, Shari gave
birth to Brandy
Cheree.

In 1980, Harry's wife, Bonnie, gave birth to Eric Anthony in Los Angeles. The family continued to live there, later moving to Pomona, California.

In 1980, Drucilla gave birth to Jerome William in Urbana, where they continued to live.

In 1981, Shari, Nancy's daughter, gave birth to Erica Rachell. The family continued to live in Springfield

In 1982, Valerie, Greg's wife, gave to birth to Carmen Renee in Sacramento.

In 1982, Katonyia, Nancy's daughter, married Frederic Thomas in Dayton, Ohio. He brought a son, Frederic (Freddie), into their marriage, whom Katonyia adopted.

In 1983, Katonyia gave birth to Felicia Antoinette in Dayton.

In 1983, Sheena gave birth to Talcum Marsh in Los Angeles. Sheena and her baby returned to Urbana.

In 1983, Jeanette gave birth to Jordon Scott in Ohio.

In 1983, Michele gave birth to Lauren.

In 1983, Chris's wife, Loretta, gave birth to Meaghan Joan in Santa Monica, California. She was raised in Gardena, California.

In 1983, Tyrin, Nancy's daughter, married Arlester Jones in Urbana.

In 1984, through Nancy's son Richie, Latasha Renee was born in Memphis, Tennessee.

In 1984, Michele gave birth to Darion Edward.

In 1984, Michael's wife, Cheryl, gave birth to twins: Marquis Dominic and Melanie Deniece in Los Angeles.

In 1984, Tyrin gave birth to Shauna Renee.

In 1985, Loretta, Chris's wife, gave birth to Patricio in Santa Monica, California. Pat was raised in Gardena, California.

In 1985, Richie,
Nancy's son, married
Lisa Rose in Las Vegas.

In 1986, Sherman's
wife, Jolene, gave
birth to Ashlee Marie
in Urbana.

In 1986, Tyrin,
Nancy's daughter,
gave birth to Michael
Devon in Urbana.

In 1986, Lisa, Richie's
wife, gave birth to
Richeena Marie at
Chanute Air Force
Base, Champaign
County, Illinois.

In 1987, Jeanette
gave birth to Erica in
Toledo, Ohio.

In 1988, Nancy's daughter Adriene married Donnell Jones in Portsmouth, Virginia. Eventually, they moved to Charlotte, North Carolina.

In 1988, Jolene, Sherman's wife, gave birth to Kellee Renee in Urbana, where the family continued to live until they later moved to Michigan.

In 1988, Sheena gave birth to Travis in Urbana, where the family continued to live.

In 1989, Annette gave birth to Joshua Lee in Los Angeles.

In 1989, Jeanette gave birth to Evan Michael in Toledo.

In 1989, Lisa, Richie's wife, gave birth to Rendal Richard III in Champaign, Illinois.

In 1990, Michael married Angel Anderson in Los Angeles

In 1990, Michael's wife, Angel, gave birth to Michael Devon in Los Angeles.

In 1990, Latosha, Annette's daughter, gave birth to Deja Nicole Manuel in Los Angeles. Afterward, Frances adopted Deja as her daughter and lived in Los Angeles until they moved to Las Vegas, Nevada.

In 1991, Tony's wife, Dawn, gave birth to Andrae in Urbana. The family later moved to Dayton.

In 1991, Chris's wife, Sabene, gave birth to Lucas Anthony in Delmenhorst, Germany. The family moved to North Carolina, and, in 2002, they moved to California.

In 1991, Annette gave birth to Tyler Alexander in Los Angeles. The family continued to live there.

In 1992, Tania, Harry's daughter, gave birth to Rahman Terrill in Los Angeles.

In 1992, Tracey, Frances's daughter, gave birth to Kyle Anthony Key in Los Angeles.

In 1992, Michael's wife, Angel, gave birth to Malcom Dewon in Los Angeles.

In 1993, Latosha, Annette's daughter, gave birth to Keiyon Reyna.

In 1993, Marcus, Harry's son, married Carrie Sananian in Los Angeles.

In 1993, Carrie, wife of Marcus, gave birth to Trevin in Los Angeles.

In 1993, Janine Adams, Michele's daughter, gave birth to Shaquil Akeem.

In 1994, Janet,
Martin's daughter,
married Colin
Richards in Charlotte,
North Carolina.

In 1994, Lisa, Richie's
wife, gave birth to
Renesha Marie in
Champaign, Illinois.

In 1995, Eric,
Katonyia's son,
married Anitra
Hughes in Urbana.

In 1995, Latosha,
Annette's daughter,
gave birth to Kierra.

In 1995, Paul married Beverly Mitchell in Urbana. That year, Paul adopted Beverly's children: Jennefer and Larry Griffith. The couple lived in the Chicago area until they moved to San Antonio.

In 1995, Tony's son Aaron married Leslie Underwood in Springfield. Aaron adopted Leslie's children: Donna and Rick Hill.

In 1995, Chris's wife, Sabene, gave birth to Tyler Robin in Fort Bragg, North Carolina. The family lived in Sanford, North Carolina, and moved to California in 2002.

In 1995, through Tony's son Andrew, Adena was born.

In 1995, Tony's son Aaron's wife, Leslie Underwood, gave birth to Eryn in Springfield.

In 1996, Leslie, Aaron's wife, gave birth to Deon in Springfield.

In 1996, Anitra, Eric's wife, gave birth to Montay, the first great-great-grandchild, in Dayton.

In 1996, Sheena married Brett Baker in Urbana.

In 1996, Jennefer, daughter of Beverly, Paul's wife, gave birth to Ebonee Phillips in Ottawa, Canada

In 1997, Tracey, Frances's daughter, married Tracy Jones in Los Angeles. He brought a daughter named Dominique Alina to the new family.

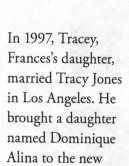

In 1997, Tracey gave birth to Kayla Noelle in Los Angeles, where the family continues to live.

In 1997, Katasha
was born through
Tony's son Andrew in
Springfield.

In 1997, Anitra, Eric's
wife, gave birth to
Eriana Lashae in
Urbana.

In 1998, Richelle,
Sheena's daughter.
married Lawrence
Williams.

In 1998, Adriene,
Nancy's daughter, and
her husband, Donnie,
adopted Brandon
Smith in Charlotte.

In 1998, Carrie, Markus' wife gave birth to Taylor.

In 1998, Latosha, Annette's daughter gave birth to Keianna Rainee in Encino, CA.

In 1998, Leslie, Aaron's wife gave birth to Karen in Springfield.

In 1999, Jennefer, daughter of Beverly, Paul's wife, gave birth to Desiree Phillips in Ottawa, Canada

In 1999, Richelle,
Sheena's daughter
gave birth to
Lawrence Jr.

In 1999, Janet,
Martin's daughter
gave birth to Janeen
Cynthia in Charlotte,
North Carolina.

In 2000, Doreen,
Martin's daughter
married Rocky Ray
in Charlotte, North
Carolina.

In 2000, Richelle,
Sheena's daughter
gave birth to Lauren
Eloyce.

In 2000, Keilyn
Ramon was born
through Scott,
Greg's son.

MARTIN S. MANUEL

In 2000, Sheree,
Sherman's daughter,
gave birth to Jayden
Daniel Wilson in
Urbana.

In 2001, Destiny
was born through
James Anthony Jr.,
nicknamed Anthony.

In 2001, Janet,
Martin's daughter,
gave birth to Jason
Christopher in
Charlotte, North
Carolina.

In 2002, Carrie, Marcus's wife, gave birth to twins: Lea and Leilani in Los Angeles.

In 2002, Adriene, Nancy's daughter, adopted Keith Jones in Charlotte.

In 2002, Alaya was born through Tony's son Andrew.

In 2002, Sheree, Sherman's daughter, married Daniel Wilson in Urbana.

In 2003, Doreen, Martin's daughter, gave birth to Charles Michael in Charlotte, North Carolina.

In 2003, Janine, Michele's daughter, gave birth to Zowey Diana.

In 2003, Isiah was born through Tony's son Andrew.

In 2004, Doreen gave birth to Martin David in Charlotte, North Carolina. The family moved to Kannapolis, North Carolina.

In 2004, Latasha, Richie's daughter and Nancy's granddaughter, gave birth to Jaylon.

In 2004, Shauna, Tyrin's daughter and Nancy's granddaughter, gave birth to Quinlon Floyd.

In 2004, Jaylyn was born through Tony's son Andrew.

In 2004, Kamarion
was born through
Anthony, Tony's son.

In 2005, Nathaniel
Crissinge was born
through Anthony,
Tony's son.

In 2005, Brandy,
Shari's daughter
and Nancy's
granddaughter,
married Joseph Irelan
in Columbus, Ohio.

In 2005, Brandy gave
birth to Braylon in
Columbus.

In 2002, Sheree,
Sherman's daughter,
gave birth to Brennan
Douglas Wilson in
Urbana.

In 2006, Carmen,
Gregory's daughter,
gave birth to Gabriel
Anthony Bell.

In 2006, Janet,
Martin's daughter,
gave birth to Jada
Cherie in Charlotte,
North Carolina.
Later, the family
moved to Redmond,
Washington.

In 2006, Erica, Shari's
daughter and Nancy's
granddaughter,
married Lloyd
M Moore III in
Columbus.

In 2007, Doreen, Martin's daughter, gave birth to Zuri Elizabeth in Kannapolis, North Carolina.

In 2002, Harry married Leanor Hernandez-Rodriquez in Los Angeles

In 2008, Anisa Lena was born through Scott, Gregory's son.

In 2009, Ashlee, Sherman's daughter, gave birth to Makiyah Jolee.

In 2009, Janine, Michele's daughter, gave birth to Asha Imani.

In 2009, Mackenzie was born through Tony's son Andrew.

In 2010, Harry's wife, Lenora, gave birth to Ryan.

In 2010, Latasha, Richie's daughter and Nancy's granddaughter, gave birth to Gerin.

In 2010, Erica Moore, Shari's daughter and Nancy's granddaughter, gave birth to Addison in Columbus, Ohio.

In 2011, Erica Moore gave birth to twins, Avery and Ayden, in Columbus.

In 2011, Kellee, Sherman's daughter, married Joel Ihrig.

In 2012, Erica Moore gave birth to twins, Ava and Ashton, in Columbus.

In 2012, Kellee, Sherman's daughter, gave birth to Jace Christopher.

In 2012, Deja Jackson, through Michael Devon, son of Michael, gave birth to Michael Devon Jr.

In 2012, Christina, Brandon's wife, gave birth to Tyler in Charlotte.

In 2013, Lauren, Michele's daughter, gave birth to Leah Marie.

In 2014, Latasha, Richie's daughter and Nancy's granddaughter, gave birth to Ayden.

In 2014, Shauna, Tyrin's daughter and Nancy's granddaughter, married Jadrice Toussaint in Charlotte.

In 2014, Shauna gave birth to Olivia in Charlotte.

In 2015, Tania, Harry's daughter, married Joseph Sinicropi.

In 2015, Richeena, Richie's daughter and Nancy's granddaughter, gave birth to twins: Jaida and Jermehle.

In 2016, Tania, Harry's daughter, gave birth to Anthony Joseph.

In 2016, Kellee, Sherman's daughter, gave birth to Jaxon.

In 2016, Ashlee, Sherman's daughter, married Justin Baylor.

In 2016, Bryce Kenneth was born through Darion, Michele's son.

In 2016, Eric, Harry's son, married Gibson Piccioli.

In 2016, Tony's granddaughter Adena gave birth to Rosie.

In 2017, Richeena, Richie's daughter and Nancy's granddaughter, gave birth to Jaliyah in Dayton.

In 2017, Lauren, Michele's daughter, gave birth to Jane.

In 2017, through Keiyon, Latosha's son and Annette's grandson, Mekhi Raimykel was born in Merced, California.

In 2017, Eric's wife, Gibson, gave birth to Francesca.

In 2018, Christina, wife of Brandon, gave birth to Skyler in Charlotte.

In 2018, Lucas Anthony, Chris's son, married Yolibeth Avena in Los Angeles.

In 2018, Erica Moore married Jeff Kirby.

In 2018, through
Kyle, Tracey's son and
Frances's grandson,
Kameron was born.

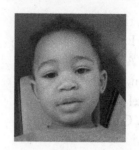

In 2018, Jordon
Carter, son of
Jeanette, married
Michele Sevia.

In 2019, through
Shaquil, Janine's
son and Michele's
grandson, Malachi
was born.

In 2019, Jordon's wife,
Michele, gave birth to
Callie Monroe.

In 2019, Melanie, Michael's daughter, married Brian Fernando in Cabrera, Dominican Republic. In 2019, Rosie Shields, through Michael Devon, Michael's son, gave birth to Nova Ty.

In 2020, Melanie, Michael's daughter, gave birth to Jael Alyvia in Washington, DC.

In 2020, Yolibeth, Lucas's wife, gave birth to Layla Junelle in Walnut Creek, California. They live in Brentwood, California.

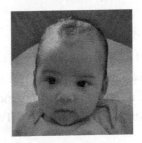

In 2020, Tyler, Chris's
daughter, married
Kevin Cudney
in Brentwood,
California. Tyler and
Kevin live in Antioch,
California.

In 2020, Felicia,
Katonyia's daughter
and Nancy's
granddaughter,
married Jason Ivey in
Atlanta, Georgia.

In 2021, Felicia,
Katonyia's daughter
and Nancy's
granddaughter, gave
birth to Harper Marie
in Atlanta, Georgia.

As of this writing, there are forty-eight grandchildren, sixty-three great-grandchildren, and twenty great-great-grandchildren. The total number of offspring, including the seventeen children not covered in this chapter, is 148. Twelve were adopted.

16

Emerging Generations

(Time period: 2011–2020)

The grandchildren and great-grandchildren of James and Florine already have started to make major marks on their communities. The stories below are of these descendants, each of whom graduated from college with degrees ranging from associate to doctorate, or they achieved exceptional results without a college degree. Also highlighted with an asterisk (*) before their names are high achievers who are not yet college age or have not yet completed their college degree programs but have exceptional résumés.

Darion Adams graduated in 2009 from the University of Georgia with a bachelor of business administration (BBA) degree in finance. He has been a licensed stockbroker since 2010, specializing in equity compensation. He transitioned to a product manager, developing an automated trading platform for clients who are eligible to set up a 10b5-1 plan. He has been working for E*TRADE since 2010, but it was acquired by Morgan Stanley, so now he works for Morgan Stanley as a senior analyst for their financial product management team.

His lifelong dream is to gain financial independence so that he can fully dictate his own schedule and how he spends his time. He plans to continue identifying various opportunities to obtain passive investments and residual income to allow money to fully work for him. His end goal is entrepreneurship.

———————

Tyrin Alston was certified at the Ohio State School of Cosmetology, and she graduated from Oklahoma City Junior College in 1993 with an associate's degree in travel and tourism. Later, she graduated from the Nancy Knight School of Nursing, with certification as a licensed practical nurse. She currently works at the Veterans Administration hospital.

———————

Kent Terry Bass retired in 2008 from the US Air Force after twenty-two years of active-duty service. His career included the Security Forces (military police) and training of K-9 units in law enforcement tactics, narcotics, and explosives detection. He was assigned to the US Secret Service to provide support to President Barack Obama and President George W. Bush. He is enrolled in Texas A&M University to complete his undergraduate degree in homeland security. He currently works for the US Air Force as an information protection specialist.

———————

Latasha Bass graduated in 2009 from Christian Brothers University with a bachelor of arts degree in psychology. She has an ongoing interest in psychology while caring full time for her children.

———————

Richeena Bass graduated from Wright State University in 2017 with an associate of applied science degree in health sciences. She maintains an interest in the health care field while caring full time for her children.

———

Richie Bass pursued his interest in law enforcement through enlisting in the US Air Force. He served for twenty years and retired as a master sergeant. In 1997, he obtained a bachelor of science degree in management studies at the University of Maryland, and in 2001, he earned a master's degree in public administration from Troy State University. Currently, he is Chief of Security and Antiterrorism in the 711ᵗʰ Human Performance Wing at Wright-Patterson Air Force Base.

———

Ashlee Baylor graduated from Washtenaw Community College with an associate of arts degree in applied science. She worked in the University of Michigan Hospital in the Transplant Center. Also, she received a certificate for "practicing attorney," based on work in a Public Defender's office. Currently, she is working on a pre-law degree, intending to become an attorney. Her dream is to advocate for patients and people.

———

Reneisha Borrero graduated in 2001 from the University of California, Berkeley, with a bachelor of science degree in civil engineering, with an emphasis on construction management. She has twenty-two years of experience in the construction industry. Her current role is Senior Project Manager with Swinerton Builders. She has completed construction projects in the San Francisco Bay area and Silicon Valley in areas such as education, commercial, affordable housing, hospitality, public works, and aviation. Currently, she is managing construction of a new middle school campus (grades 6–8) valued at $85 million, which is part of the largest K–12 education project throughout California.

She seeks to develop a successful general contracting business, specializing in home recording studios

Erica Carter graduated from Otterbein University in 2009 with a bachelor of arts degree, having majored in organizational communications with a minor in public speaking. In 2011, Erica received a master's degree at Keller Graduate School of Management in project management. She has been employed with the Department of Defense for over twelve years. At the same time, she is actively involved in her church and participated in her church website video "Living Single," in which she gives guidance to singles of all ages.

Evan Carter graduated from Xavier University in 2011 with a bachelor of arts degree; he majored in public relations and minored in political science and strategic human resources. He has worked as a manager at Abercrombie and Nationwide Insurance as an attorney negotiator.

Tyler Cudney graduated in 2019 from the University of San Francisco with a bachelor's degree in English. She also earned her master's degree in education from the University of San Francisco in 2020, with summa cum laude honors. She is currently a first-year teacher of fifth grade at John Muir Elementary School in Antioch, California.

Her goal as a teacher is to create a safe space for her students, where optimal learning can occur. A large part of her teaching philosophy is inquiry-based learning. She is working on creating lessons that make students curious and excited to learn. While she wants learning to be fun, she also has high expectations for her students to do their best work.

———————————

Shari Eubanks earned an associate in applied science degree and received her registered nurse (RN) credentials from Sinclair Community College in 1988. There, she worked on a school committee to bring in more funding for the clinical classrooms and labs. While working at Mercy Medical Center, she taught open heart classes at the hospital to educate more RNs on taking care of heart patients, before and after surgery.

She established Healing Hope, aspiring to educate and coach senior citizens toward individual wellness.

———————————

Jennefer Belle Griffith graduated from Willis Business College in 1996 with a diploma in accounting. She was Marketing Coordinator at National Seafood Sector. In 2012, National Seafood Sector was rebranded as Food Processing Skills Canada, where she was promoted to executive director in 2014.

———————————

Melanie Fernando graduated with a bachelor of science degree in health sciences in 2007 and a master of science degree in occupational therapy (MSOT) in 2009. Early in her career, she worked at the Atlanta VA Medical Center, where she obtained training to specialize in treatment of patients with upper-extremity trauma and dysfunction. Also, she worked with patients suffering from physical and neurological conditions caused by impairments of the brain and spinal cord.

She combined her career with her love of travel as a traveling occupational therapist (OT) in several states, where she worked in acute care, ICU, home health, skilled nursing facilities, outpatient rehab, and other settings.

Currently, she is a senior OT in an outpatient rehab clinic, primarily treating patients with varying postsurgical and repetitive strain injury diagnoses. She is STAR certified for oncology rehab, as well as LSVT BIG certified, specializing in treatment of patients with Parkinson's disease.

She has always had a passion for event planning, staging, and execution, so she plans to obtain training and establish a business in this field.

---

* *Makiyah Hopkins*, ten-year-old daughter of Justin and Ashlee Baylor, was elected president of her class at Heritage Elementary School and has served in that role for two years. She has led an initiative to upgrade her school playground to what she calls Generation Z Playground, which she envisions will be an example for new and upgraded playgrounds nationwide. She aspires to be president of the United States.

Kellee Ihrig graduated in 2015 from Western Michigan University with an associate of registered nursing (RN) degree, and in 2020, she graduated from Ohio University with a bachelor of science nursing (BSN) degree. She has worked as a surgical ICU RN in Charge and Rapid Response RN and as an ACLS instructor for ICU nurses, as well as new residents and physicians. In 2018, she was a Daisy Award winner, which honors nurses internationally for exemplifying high nursing values and for demonstrating excellence in patient care.

Braylon Irelan, fourteen-year-old son of Brandy Mabra, is a high school freshman at Lake Norman Charter School, Huntersville, North Carolina, and member of the National Honor Society. He studies in advanced classes of science and math and plays AAU and high school basketball. He enjoys helping younger kids play basketball, and he collaborates with coaches during the play of the game. He has dreams of playing basketball at Duke University.

Dr. Felicia Ivey graduated with her bachelor of science degree in exercise physiology from the Ohio State University in 2005; she obtained a master's degree in occupational therapy from Brenau University in 2014 and completed her doctorate in occupational therapy degree from Chatham University in 2020. She is a doctor of occupational therapy who is currently part of a regional leadership team to develop all new hires and provide clinical education to therapists within her region.

She hopes to use her background and education to eventually start her own health care consulting company and found a nonprofit that grants scholarships for diverse students to pursue degrees in the allied health field, while reducing the student loan crisis. Her dream is to remain healthy and humble and to have freedom during her day to spend time with family and friends.

Adriene Jones is a 2005 graduate of Austin Peay State University, Clarksville, Tennessee, with an associate of science degree. She has used her education to further the education and development of health maintenance senior centers.

Michael Jones holds a bachelor of science degree in computer forensics and received a master's degree in 2016 in information security. Currently, he is working on his doctorate degree.

Erica Kirby received a bachelor of arts degree in mass communication from the Ohio State University in 2004, and she received a master of business administration (MBA) degree from Franklin University in 2007. She enjoys writing and authored a book in 2018; she plans on pursuing her love of the craft as a full-time endeavor.

Brandy Mabra graduated from the Ohio State University with a bachelor of science degree in 2002. She earned a master's degree in health administration from A. T. Still University in 2014. She has used her education to work in upper management and start her own business, working with entrepreneurs by providing business and leadership coaching and training.

She has been recognized as a leader and has been published in various publications, as well as featured in numerous podcasts. Her dream in life is to make an impact on the world by using her God-given leadership gift to help and inspire others and to be a role model to her son.

Aaron Manuel earned an associate of applied science degree in industrial technology at Clark State Community College in 2002. In 2004, he earned a bachelor of science degree in technical management from Franklin University. In 2008, he earned a master of business administration degree from the Ohio State University, Fisher College of Business.

At Honda R&D, as a test equipment engineer, he led teams on $50 million of various technical projects. While working for STAN Solutions, he led a team that completed fifty-six separately permitted restoration projects for Greater Dayton. These projects won several renewal awards. He is currently Deputy Director of Construction for the Ohio Statehouse, overseeing a $20 million project, the largest since the early 1990's restoration.

Andrae Manuel graduated from the Community College of the Air Force in 2015, with a certificate in the National Registry of Emergency Medical Technicians. The same year, he graduated from the University of Cincinnati with a bachelor of arts degree in organizational leadership. In 2021, he graduated from Indiana Wesleyan University, with a master of business administration degree.

He has worked as an aide to Senator Sherrod Brown, in multiple temporary duty assignments and deployment as medical technician for the US Air Force, in hospitals, in ER units, and in ambulances as a National Registered Emergency Medical Technician (EMT). He served as NCOIC/Flight Sergeant of the Wright-Patterson Air Force Base Honor Guard.

He has ambitions to start his own business and is taking the steps toward starting a logistics company and securing a partnership with Amazon.

Deon Manuel graduated from the University of Cincinnati in 2019 with a bachelor of science degree in electrical engineering. He intends to work in control engineering, writing code for electrical and electronic devices. From childhood, he always wanted to be an engineer; he always was taking things apart to learn how they worked.

———————————•◆•———————————

Eric Manuel received his bachelor of science degree in civil engineering from Arizona State University in 2003. He went on to complete his master of business administration degree in 2006 from the University of Phoenix. In 2007, he enlisted in the US Navy Reserves and made the rank of E5 (Petty Officer, Second Class). After four years of enlisted service, he went on to apply for officer programs with the US Navy Civil Engineer Corps. He spent six years with the US Navy Seabees, where he reached the rank of lieutenant (O-3), with ten years of service. He currently works as an engineering manager at a large engineering firm headquartered in Tucson, Arizona. His educational background in civil engineering has afforded him the opportunity to work on many prestigious projects, which include some of the world's most advanced astronomical observatories.

His dream is to work toward starting a successful business and becoming more involved in charity.

———————————•◆•———————————

Lucas Manuel began his military service in 2011, serving as a signal support systems specialist. In 2013, two years after enlistment in the army, he was selected for an ROTC scholarship and attended the University of San Francisco, where he majored in international studies, with a concentration on peace and conflicts, and a minor in Latin American studies. He was commissioned as a second lieutenant to serve in the army as a military police officer and received a bachelor's degree in 2016.

He was later hired as a police officer in the city of Berkeley, California, and graduated from the Alameda County Sheriff's

Academy in 2018. After a short time on patrol, he deployed to Guantanamo Bay, Cuba, in 2018. During his deployment, he oversaw 105 soldiers to run a federal detention facility. He is currently an operations officer in the 357th Military Police Company. After his deployment from Guantanamo Bay, he decided to change careers from a police officer to a cyber-security professional. He is seeking a second degree in software engineering, where he plans to combine his law enforcement background with cyber security to get into computer forensics investigation.

————————————————

Meaghan Onli received a bachelor's degree in fine arts from the School of the Art Institute of Chicago and her master's degree in art history from one of the most prestigious art schools in the world, the Courtauld Institute of Art in London, England. She is an accomplished artist, public speaker, writer, and curator. She is currently the assistant curator at the Institute of Contemporary Art at the University of Pennsylvania.

Before joining the Institute of Contemporary Art, she worked for the Graham Foundation for Advanced Studies in the Fine Arts, where she worked on the exhibitions *African Modernism* and *Barbara Kasten and Architecture of Independence.* She is responsible for creating the website Black Visual Archive in 2010. She received the Creative Capital Warhol Foundation Arts Writers Grant in 2012. She was also a recipient of a research grant from the Graham Foundation for *Remaking the Black Metropolis: Contemporary Art, Urbanity, and Blackness in America*, with curator Jamilee Polson Lacy.

————————————————

Malcolm Manuel graduated from Golden West College with an associate of arts degree in social and behavioral science in 2013 and from Montana State University–Northern (MSUN) with a bachelor of science degree in health promotion in 2016.

As a student, he was an intern on the MSUN coaching staff for a year, coaching the running backs and assisting in the redshirt lifting program. Afterward, he moved back to California, coaching track-and-field at Banning High School, taking the team to the Los Angeles City Relay championship for the first time in eighteen years and taking the next two years, making it three consecutive appearances during his tenure.

While at Banning High School, he also coached JV football and, after three seasons, the varsity team. At the age of twenty-seven, in July 2020, he was announced as the head football coach at Narbonne High School in Harbor City, California, one of the most storied and prolific programs in the state of California.

His next goal is to obtain a master's degree in both sports administration and sports psychology. His long-term goal is to coach at the highest level, the NFL.

Michael Devon Manuel graduated from the University of California, Berkeley (UC Berkeley), in 2013 with a bachelor of arts degree in American studies, with an emphasis in architecture. There, he played on the football team in his junior and senior seasons. At UC Berkeley he achieved Academic All-American honors and won the Ken Harvey Award. He developed a love for coaching, mentoring, training, and, eventually, community service relations.

Shortly after graduating, he worked for Enterprise and Milwaukee Tools. Afterward, he started the Greek Town Apparel Company, using his love for design concepts in a local and online retail store. With a passion to help and to grow his community, he has also started a grassroots organization called the Black Father's Project in Los Angeles, which focuses on the black father through community resources and workshops.

He became a certified personal trainer and has worked with people of all demographics. His passion is working with the youth, but he enjoys all ages. He is currently working on building a company that will connect neighborhood communities and trainers, locally and, eventually, regionally. Currently, he is a strength-and-conditioning coach in Los Angeles.

Michael's dream is to become a serial entrepreneur in multiple industries. He is currently working on attaining his certification as a strength-and-conditioning specialist through the National Collegiate Sports Association. His goal is to continue to coach athletes and eventually own his own facility, where he will train privately and help others build their careers.

———

Patricio Manuel graduated from Santa Monica Community College in 2006 with an associate's degree in liberal arts. Pat is also a five-time female National Amateur Boxing champion. Pat began boxing at age thirteen, with his last fight as a female in 2012 at the Olympic trials, where he withdrew after a shoulder injury. He became a professional male boxer and fought Hugo Aguilar in December 2018. He won by unanimous decision, becoming the first transgender female-to-male boxer to defeat a male professional boxer.

He is an LBGTQ rights spokesman. In 2019, he became the face for Everlast's Be First campaign. He trains others while training for his next professional featherweight fight. He is also an entrepreneur, an online personal trainer, a social entrepreneur wellness coach, and a stress-management specialist. He owns Dark Horse, a digital marketing company.

———

Katonyia Parks graduated from Southwestern College of Dayton, Ohio, with a bachelor of arts in accounting in 1992. She ran three businesses for more than sixteen years.

———

Doreen Ray graduated from Ambassador University in 1996 with a bachelor of science degree in family consumer science, with a concentration in family studies and a minor in Christian studies. She works at Cornerstone Baptist Church of Charlotte as the children's ministry director and volunteers as the troop shepherd for American Heritage Girls. She has a passion for teaching and mentoring children from a young age, and this has been a theme for much of her life, including homeschooling her three children. She loves making music and has devoted many years to praising God in worship. She makes one or two trips a year to serve as a missionary in Haiti and is on the board of a nonprofit that provides jobs, education, clean water, and other assistance in that country. Her dream is to make a difference in the lives of her children and the other children she works with in her church and in Haiti.

Latosha Reyna earned an associate in arts degree in behavioral science from LA Harbor College in 2015. In 2017, she earned a bachelor of arts degree in sociology, with a minor in African American studies, from the University of California, Los Angeles (UCLA). In 2019, she earned a master of social work degree from the University of Southern California. Currently, she works for Hope of the Valley as a housing navigator, providing intensive-case management and finding stable and permanent homes for families. Before Hope of the Valley, she worked for California State University, Long Beach, Upward Bound program as a program coordinator, supporting and developing needy young people.

Her dream is to earn a doctoral degree in social work, become a licensed clinical therapist, and start her own nonprofit that provides resources, services, and support for victims of sexual assault and domestic and interpersonal violence, as well as victims of trafficking, including commercially sexually exploited children and youth.

———————— ‡•♦•‡ ————————

Janeen Richards is a 2019 graduate of Bellevue College with an associate of arts and sciences degree and currently is a student at Oregon State University, working toward a bachelor of arts (BA) degree in cultural and linguistic anthropology. While working on her classes online, she is studying language and culture in Turkey, intending to complete her BA and eventually a master of arts degree. Her dream is to continue to pursue language learning and become a polyglot and apply linguistic anthropology to her life and work wherever she lives. Also, she seeks to continue to use her singing and music, especially in worship, to express her love for Christ in any setting.

———————— ‡•♦•‡ ————————

Janet Richards graduated from Ambassador University in 1991 with a bachelor of arts degree, having majored in management information systems and minored in theology. She had a twenty-two-year career at Microsoft Corporation and a five-year career as a consultant, including starting Janet Richards Consulting, LLC. She is a certified project management professional.

She was a co-lead in starting an online international church community. She was appointed Human Services Commissioner for Redmond, Washington, in 2019. She serves as chair of Seattle Children's Hospital's Family Advisory Board. She is a founding member of Right to Breath, an organization working with the Seattle Eastside communities on civil rights for black people.

Her dream is to create spiritually healthy communities through Jesus Christ. She is starting a nonprofit organization that will provide services through the Christian community to the greater Redmond region, as well as serve as the financial arm of the Gather congregation (also in the process of forming). She is working on her pastoral credentials, with the goal of becoming an ordained pastor.

———————— ◆◆◆ ————————

Shauna Toussaint earned a bachelor of science in nursing (BSN) degree from Wright State University in 2007 and a master of science in nursing (MSN) degree from the University of Phoenix in 2012. She is a registered nurse (RN) and owns a health care consulting business. She also holds a realtor's license and has received national recognition and training as a senior real estate specialist (SRES).

Her experience in the health care sector helped her cultivate market sense and see the big picture in helping to meet the special needs of maturing adults. Her primary focus is to make sure she provides an excellent experience as her clients enter the next phase of life. Shauna loves spending time with her family, traveling, and decorating homes.

———————— ◆◆◆ ————————

* *Lauren Eloyce Williams* graduated from Rochester Adams High School, Rochester Hills, Michigan, in 2019 with a 3.95 GPA; she is currently a student at Hampton University. She has shadowed the Honorable Cynthia Thomas Walker in the Fiftieth District Court in Pontiac, Michigan, attentively listening to court hearings. She garnered awards in high school, including the Dean's List and Scholar of Distinction, as well as earning a Hampton University merit scholarship. She also earned the 2019 Freddye T. Davy Freshman Honors. She operates her own business and YouTube channel.

Her dream is to become a criminal defense attorney and to one day open her own law firm. Her education at Hampton University will help to prepare her for the LSAT and law school overall, as she is on the pre-law track.

———————— ◆◆◆ ————————

Richelle Williams is a 1998 graduate of Wright State University, Dayton, Ohio, with a bachelor of arts degree in psychology. She also has certification in therapeutic recreation and has worked in the social services, mental health, and health care fields. Her passion for working with seniors became personal when she watched her grandfather, who had worked seven days a week, go back and forth between the hospital and nursing home for six months. It gave her a new appreciation for the seasoned residents with whom she works.

Her goal is to become an executive director of an assisted living community.

Sheree Wilson graduated from DeVry University with a bachelor of arts degree in technical management. She works for Catholic Services with people in need. Her two programs are long-term recovery in the low-income areas that were severely damaged by tornados that struck Dayton in 2019, and assistance for those assigned to supervised visits, to give children a place that is safe and friendly. Also, she serves in a food pantry.

Her work to help people in need fulfills a passion that she acquired after her own life-changing health crisis.

These brief summaries of thirty-nine descendants and one adopted stepchild, all exceptional contributors, exemplify the legacy of James and Florine Manuel. Several of them are now retired, but most of them have their careers ahead of them. That such an impressive list stems from two people speaks volumes about their grandparents.

17

FAITH

(Time period: 1919–forever)

The name *Manuel* is biblical, derived from the Hebrew word *Immanuel*, which means "God with us." Whether a name is inherited, transferred, or given, it often has significant meaning. Although James and Florine did not attempt to impose the significance of this name on their children, time has shown that the name has identified them—not all immediately but one at a time—so that as of this writing, most—if not all—of the children identify with God, both in belief and in prayer.

Faith is a personal and individual thing. This chapter is about the individual faith of James and Florine and the faith of their children. In addition, this chapter discusses faith in the Manuel nuclear family and the collective faith that increasingly is expressed in the families of the children.

James and Florine and every one of their children have shown consistent expressions of belief in God. Those expressions, however, vary greatly in many ways.

Florine's faith was established in her childhood through her mother, Phoebe, a Catholic from her childhood. Florine intended to raise her children in the Catholic faith, and the early schooling of her first two children in St. Raphael School started them on that path. Because of the cost of private education, she later consented to public education for all of the children by the time the third child started school.

Florine was a devout member of St. Joseph Catholic Church near her childhood residence. This was the church that helped the family during James's unemployment in the late 1950s. In spite of the financial need, Florine found a way to donate, even if no more than a dollar, to Catholic missions. In spite of her responsibilities to her family, she served the priests of St. Joseph Church, ironing their ecclesiastical outer garments so that they were ready for the Mass. Although she and James collaborated in naming their children, she always preferred names of saints as either the first or middle name.

After the family moved to Harrison Street in 1963, Florine enrolled the younger children in St. Joseph Catholic School. This continued until the move to Urbana in 1966, at which time St. Mary School became the choice for the younger ones. All of the younger Manuel children, however, completed their education in Urbana public schools.

James did not affiliate with any church, but he believed in God. He prayed on his knees regularly and believed that Christians should live according to their faith. He did not respect people who professed faith in God through church membership but behaved in ways that were inconsistent with their professing. Although he thought as he did, according to his words to one of his children, he did not intend to make a personal commitment to any church membership. Understandably, he did not require any of the children to profess to or have association with religion.

Although they experienced the Catholic catechism in school, the first few Manuel children tended to express their faith more like James than Florine. They were reserved, not discussing their religious beliefs but praying regularly. Both Nancy and Frances tried to live respectably and practice love for each other. After living in California, Frances associated with the Catholic Church there and then in Las Vegas.

Martin, who Florine enrolled in Catholic catechism when he was fourteen, was the first of the children to affiliate with a church of his own choice while living at home in Springfield. He had been curious about God at around age eight and was concerned about living in obedience. But it was ten years later when God got his attention during the Cuban Missile Crisis. Martin came home from work and asked his mom if he could borrow her Bible, which was the Douay-Rheims version in English. When he opened it, the stunning words before his eyes were of Jesus talking about the end of the world! From then on, he became a regular reader of the Bible and began to seek God, although he didn't attend a church. At first, his departure from the Catholic Church, followed by affiliation with another church, was not well received by Florine, who wanted to preserve the Catholic participation of all the children. James, however, supported Martin, insisting that he and all the others were free to choose their faith. Although his faith was initially triggered by fear, Martin came to understand the love of God for him and the role of Jesus as Savior in dispensing that love for all people, including him. This led him to an ongoing relationship with God. He devoted himself to service through his church and eventually became a church pastor and author of Christian books.

In Urbana, Drucilla, Sheena, Sherman, Tony, and Michele got involved in a youth program at a church there. They attended a revival at the Hill Street AME church and became part of the Gospel Prophets singing group. The priest at St. Mary Catholic Church criticized their attendance in another church, so all of the children left St. Mary and attended that church, which the children considered more relevant than the repetitious activities of the Catholic Mass. The Gospel Prophets was a valuable experience for young people. Forty young members of the group traveled from place to place to sing. Jeanie Gordon and her husband, Richard, taught and related well to the teenagers in the group. At the same time, they insisted on discipline and taught the youths how to conduct themselves.

This experience had lasting effects on the faith of the five Manuel children who participated.

Years earlier, Florine had prayed for her first set of twins, Sheena and Sherman, when they were infants and severely ill, promising in faith to dedicate them to God. Sherman started showing interest in God at an early age. Around then, he experienced a miraculous escape from injury in an automobile accident. He had received Jesus as his Savior at the Hill Street AME Church revival. Later, when he was in California, he was involved in another auto accident, being struck broadside and seriously injured. When he regained consciousness, he prayed that God would spare him and promised to devote his life to service. One night, while at his brother's house, recovering from the accident, he experienced a surge of joy and found himself healed. Sherman felt a close relationship with God during the worst of his troubles. All of this prompted him to return to Urbana and start a youth center. Several years later, he was baptized, strengthening his faith. Sherman has continued to be an active member of his church and in community service.

Sheena, likewise, responded early in life to God's call. While a senior in high school, she responded to an altar call by coming forward. There, she experienced what she described as a charismatic manifestation of the Holy Spirit. Later, after she was married, she had a similar experience. At a church service, a minister, who did not know her, told her not to worry about her daughter; Sheena had been worried about her at the time. She considers these events to be confirmations of her faith. She continues as a regular member of her church in Urbana.

Michele recalls reading the Bible more with the Hill Street AME Church than with the Catholic Church. She learned about God and prayer. During the Catholic Mass, she knew what to do, but it didn't mean anything. Faith has been a continual part of her life, which has included tragedies, but she has seen Jesus, in her words, "move mountains." At the same time, she has had some negative experiences in church. A pastor in St. Louis offended her by criticizing her fur coat. In another church, she was so involved in ministries that it became overwhelming. She felt exhausted from never-ending requests to expend her time in church service.

Jeanette attended St. Mary Catholic Church in Urbana with her family. At the age of nine, she experienced curiosity about God and realized that the Catholic Church did not give her answers. For unexplained reasons, life became difficult for her in her mid-teens. It was around then that she traveled to Chicago to spend the summer with her brother and his family there, and while visiting, she attended church services where many other teens worshipped. It changed her life. When she returned home, she experienced the presence of the Lord in her room. She informed Florine about her new faith and desire to leave the Catholic Church, but her mom was not receptive. Jeanette reacted angrily, which necessitated her moving out of her parents' home to live with a sister. There, she continued to experience God's presence and protection, even when an intruder broke into her apartment. Later, while in California, she was taking a shower when she experienced the Holy Spirit moving her to speak in tongues. At age twenty-one, she moved back to Ohio, and in Columbus, with her husband's sisters, she visited churches. Jeanette has been an active member in her church and participant in several ministries as well as working as a full-time employee in the church administration.

Annette watched her twin sister, Jeanette, and she noticed her faith and special relationship with Christ at a young age. She wanted the same, but it took years before her heart was touched to accept Jesus. She was baptized in 2010. She sees her life as more than an attempt to do good deeds; Christ is her personal Savior. Looking back, she can see that God had a hand on her all of her life. The opportunities she got without asking and the doors that opened for her convinced her that God loves her. The year that her job was downsized was difficult. She asked her husband to help at a time of financial need, as she had helped him, but instead, he left her. Nonetheless, God has taken care of her. Although the past year has been difficult, she considers it a good year. Even in retirement, every step has been guided by God.

Chris was intrigued by the Trinity and has always seen his faith side as a third part of him. At times, he has felt special protection; for example, when a mine blew up near him, he was unharmed. The enemy in Afghanistan had a contract on him, but he experienced a "ring of security" around him. He believes that he has received many blessings that he does not deserve. The prayers of others put him in position and gave him opportunities. He realizes that James and Florine prayed for him because they worried that he would go the wrong way in his life. Their prayers were answered.

Tony explained the role of the Gospel Prophets singing group in his faith. He said the Gospel Prophets were a spinoff from the Black Brothers and Sisters in Urbana; in the late 1960s, Urbana had a great deal of racial unrest. The only way for him and many others to deal with it was to be in a group. He joined the group in 1970. Also, he and Sherman sang with an R&B group called Soul Enterprise. They sang at dances, and that was a bridge to the Gospel Prophets. He was saved when he was with the Gospel Prophets, part of the AME Church in Urbana. Today, he does not belong to an organized church, but he has started reading and is part of small-group studies.

"Faith plays a huge role in my life," said Greg. He is not a church member and does not like priests and pastors because of their inconsistency in living as they profess. He believes in God, and God has always been in his life. He has seen miracles. For example, when he and his wife, Valerie, wanted to buy a house, they needed $30,000 to qualify for financing. Their plans seemed to fail, but then Valerie received a check in the mail for $17,000 as a payout from her insurance company. Four days later, Greg received a check for$13,000. Within a week, they had received exactly what they needed and were able to proceed to purchase the house. Greg has always tried to help others, and he has noticed that his gifts "come back tenfold." He experienced premonitions when his life was in danger while serving as a law enforcement officer.

Paul, throughout his life, has always prayed. When it comes to learning, he tends to go on gut feelings rather than academic knowledge. As a track team participant, from the time he was a nine-year-old in elementary school through a twenty-two-year-old college student, he has prayed before pole vaulting. Early in his life, Catholicism influenced his faith, but as he grew older, he realized that Catholicism was not for him.

An example of the role of faith in his life took place in Iraq, when, as a US Army soldier, he was with his unit, preparing for the ground war. An artillery truck caught fire. Realizing the extreme danger of exploding artillery and such, he and the other soldiers frantically worked to put out the fire, and when they failed, they moved the truck away from the camp. Although the soldiers were unhurt, the truck exploded, causing extensive damage to the camp. That night, as he thought about the damaged base camp, he cried out, "What am I doing here?" He explains that, in answer, God told him exactly what he was to do: speak to his sister Michele about a job, go to school, and gain expertise in electronics. When he was discharged, he followed the instructions that he considers a plan: moving to Chicago, consulting with Michele, and studying at the Consumer Electronic Training Center. His degree in electronics led to a job. His eventual move from Chicago to San Antonio was similar.

Harry believes that he has a guardian angel looking after him. That belief, as well as the realization of something greater than him involved in his life, gives him purpose and inner strength.

Michael experienced racism in Catholic school, which hurt his self-esteem. After he moved to Los Angeles, he joined Faithful Central Missionary Baptist Church in Englewood. There, he had an unexpected charismatic experience that triggered a deep interest in God. Job stress caused chest pain that put him in a hospital for three days. Advised by medical staff not to return to work immediately, he traveled to Africa, where he encountered another charismatic experience and became convinced of his purpose and passion in life—community outreach. The churches he attended, however, were not interested in outreach, so God opened the door for him to serve in the community through an unexpected invitation to teach in the Dayton Public Schools (DPS). The DPS facility in which he now works has all the equipment and tools for him to accomplish his desire to serve his community.

Although this chapter focuses on the faith of James, Florine, and their children, much could be added about the faith of the third-generation members of the family and beyond. Already among them are God-fearing people and devoted Christians. Some serve as church leaders or church planters, ministers, and missionaries. Perhaps their stories will be told in a future edition of this book. The stories below are about four of these family members. Because of their unique experiences that involved their faith, they have notable—if not amazing—accounts that throw light on the extent of faith in the family, which is why they are shared here.

One of the most memorable times of faith in the family occurred around the time of Florine's illness in 2011, when one of her great-grandchildren became seriously ill. Jason Richards, ten-year-old son of Janet and Colin Richards and Martin's grandson, experienced a cardiac arrest while undergoing a routine heart catheterization in Seattle, Washington. Jason was born with a defective heart and had previously undergone several critical lifesaving surgeries to enable him to enjoy a quality life while somewhat physically impaired. The 2011 event nearly took his life and necessitated a heart transplant for him to continue to live. The family members, joined by friends and fellow believers, prayed for Jason's survival. Repeatedly, those prayers were answered; after three months in the hospital and over a year after discharge, he lived on with the defective heart while remaining on the transplant list for a matching heart. In late 2012, he received a transplanted heart, but his health struggles did not end then. In 2013, just after his isolation to protect his compromised immune system, he contracted Legionnaires' disease, which damaged his lungs and required seven more months of hospitalization.

Jason received a new heart by transplant
shortly after this photo was taken.

Miraculously, Jason recovered, astonishing his doctors. For the
next four years, he underwent procedure after procedure to diagnose
and correct a problem of excessive pressure on the right side of his
heart. Eventually, his doctors concluded that his heart would fail,
and because the failure was caused by a chronic condition apart
from his heart, he would not be eligible for another heart transplant.
In 2017, Jason was granted his wish through the Make-A-Wish
Foundation, which was to have his close family members spend a
week with him. Because he could not travel, his family members
from North Carolina traveled to a week-long celebration with him
in his home. But instead of steadily declining through heart failure,
which was his prognosis, Jason grew stronger. Early in 2020, his
doctors declared him free of chronic pulmonary hypertension, a
condition that they had said was incurable. Space here does not
permit the details of the many miracles that preserved Jason's life,
but they are documented in *Dear Jason*,[5] a Kindle book written by
his grandfather Martin.

---

[5] Martin S. Manuel, *Dear Jason* (Amazon Kindle, 2013).

About twelve years earlier, another miracle occurred that involved the birth of Cecelia Jeanette Carter's baby, Evan. Here is the faith story, told by Jeanette:

At thirteen weeks, my amniotic fluid prematurely erupted, leaving me standing in a pool of fluid. This pregnancy was my fourth, so I soon realized that my water had broken. I immediately informed my husband, and off we went to Toledo Hospital. The doctors informed us that in twenty-four hours, I would go into spontaneous labor, and the chances of survival for our baby were slim to none. I was on complete bed rest for twenty-two weeks while the amniotic fluid continued to spill out, twenty-four/ seven. On August 14, 1989, a miracle occurred, and our son Evan Michael Carter was born at thirty-five weeks, weighing four pounds fourteen ounces.

Evan's survival is miraculous! He was born with only half a cup of amniotic fluid, which left him with hyaline membrane disease of the lungs. He required ventilator pressures of 50/5 and 100 percent oxygen. Eventually, the doctors had to increase the ventilator to 90 percent pressure. We were told that his lungs would rupture if this continued. God was in control, and after twenty days of oxygen, Evan was able to breathe on his own.

At birth, his diagnosis was a heart murmur and club feet, which required casts for the first year of his life. His spine was curved, and he would have to wear a front/back brace for five years, but God healed Evan's body completely. The doctors said he might have brain damage from his premature birth and might not be able to walk. "If It Had Not Been for the Lord on [Our] Side"! We are truly grateful that God has the final say.

Evan, at about age five. His name is the Welsh version of John, meaning "God is gracious."

Evan has grown into a fine young man, whose outstanding contributions are mentioned in chapter 16, "Emerging Generations."

A third story about God's grace is about Ashlee Manuel, daughter of Sherman and Jolene Manuel. Her dad tells it:

> Born on April 11, 1986, Ashlee was one child who always had a smile on her face. Even when she was disciplined, she would still have that contagious smile.
>
> I took her to California to see my dad in 1986. She sat on my lap the entire time on the flight and people were amazed how good she was; she just smiled at them. She lit up the room when my dad saw her.

Speaking of Deddy, I recall him coming home from a hard day of work from the foundry, and he would lie on the floor because his back was out of place. He would have us walk on his back for pain relief. The next day he would head off to work, back pain and all.

I too had several back surgeries, and so did some of my brothers. It can be a debilitating and painful experience. I never thought bad back problems would be handed down to any of my daughters.

Some twenty years ago, Ashlee was visiting friends. She walked out onto a rear porch and, without realizing it, stepped into a hole in the porch. Her leg went through the hole all the way up to her thigh. From that point forward, for the next twenty years, she underwent numerous failed back surgeries. Imagine her twenty years of debilitating pain, yet she still had that smile.

Ashlee would be the first to tell you that it was only by the grace of God that she was able to endure this pain and even go on to have a healthy child when the doctors had told her that she couldn't. Yes, indeed, God is good all the time, through sickness, pain, and health.

This is Ashlee when she was a little girl, always
lighting up the space and people around her.

We cannot take life for granted because we never
know when we or a family member could have
an accident that could alter having a normal life.
Regardless, Ashlee would tell you to focus on God
and his goodness, and because of Him regardless
of your pain and suffering, He will help you keep a
smile on your face.

Marquis, Michael's first son, died in 2008 at the age of twenty-
five in a swimming accident. In his short life, he demonstrated his
faith while working on a cruise ship as a chef and later settling in St
Augustine, Florida, where he continued his profession. After work,
he would shower and then take the food that was left over to feed
the homeless. He was a street preacher who believed in the power of
prayer and practiced that belief in his service to the needy.

Besides being a chef, a graduate from Le Cordon Bleu College
of Culinary Arts in San Francisco, where he was awarded
a trip to Paris, France, Marquis was an expert swimmer.
Also, he was a musician, releasing a gospel-rap album that
involved Grammy award–winning artist Keith Harrison.

From the various stories of personal faith, we see a common
thread, as well as wide differences. The common thread is that
the Manuel family unanimously believes in the existence of God.
To each of them, God is a personal being who has been and still
is involved in their lives. He cares about them, protects them, and
blesses them. All of them pray to God. We can think of such people
as God-fearing.

The Bible talks about God-fearing people. One example is
Cornelius, a Roman centurion. The story is found in chapter 10 of
the book of Acts. It might seem odd that a military official, stationed
in an administration center of the Roman Empire, would acquire
the belief of the Jewish people about God and not only believe but
practice faith by praying and doing good deeds. Cornelius's entire
family shared his faith. The story does not say what he and his family
members expected of God, but their actions are evidence that they
lived their lives in faith in the one true God, not in worship of one
of the pagan deities common among Romans.

The heartwarming outcome of the story is that God noticed their worship and rewarded them by opening the opportunity for them to know Him even more deeply and experience His ultimate intentions toward them. God likes to bless people, but He has a relationship in mind. He wants us to embrace His forgiveness of sins and gift of eternal life through believing in Jesus Christ. The Cornelius story showcases the destiny of the God-fearing person.

Some members of the Manuel family have taken the step of responding to the call of that destiny. These members have accepted Jesus Christ as their Savior, committed their lives to following Him, and embarked upon an ongoing relationship with God the Father and Jesus Christ through the Holy Spirit.

Why mention faith in this biography? The simple answer is that without faith, there would be no story. *Manuel Strong* is about an extraordinary group of people, and, according to each of them, the true narrative of their lives is powered by God. Leave this belief out of the story and the extraordinary outcome has no explanation.

CONCLUSION

This book asserts that an ordinary African American couple, in spite of unreasonable obstacles, realized a legacy of extraordinary accomplishments in their personal lives and through their progeny. The story of this family contradicts the stereotypes of black people in the United States of America. *Manuel Strong: The Life and Legacy of James and Florine Manuel* is not an attempt to boast about individuals or a family. The truth in these pages should enlighten readers in this country and elsewhere. James and Florine Manuel never boasted about their accomplishments. Both of them were extremely modest people who tried to do their best but realized that they were ordinary folks. In telling their story after their deaths, the faith statements of their children clearly attribute the actual credit to God. It was God who gave each and all of them the desire to achieve, and He supplies the drive to pursue the desire. God blesses, opening doors of opportunity. God helps in time of need, especially when such help is requested. God rescues from trouble and disaster. Only He knows how often James and Florine asked and even pleaded for these very things.

Readers of this story will come away with various viewpoints and opinions, but those of us who share this story hope that many will understand this pivotal truth: all human beings, regardless of their nationalities or ethnicities, through application of the desire and drive created in them and faith in the God who is with them, can achieve great things, in spite of the obstacles they encounter.

Our desire is that those who tend to package black people in a box of negative stereotypes realize that they have it all wrong. Black people are like all other people. Some are industrious, and some are not. Some may even be lazy. But until their actual accomplishments are considered in the context of the playing field upon which they must compete, the judgmental measures of them are usually inaccurate.

Our hope is that any people who limit themselves because of their disadvantages, whatever they are, might find encouragement of what patient application of desire and drive—along with faith in the God who gives and supports them—can produce in the long run. In the same way, our longing is that people who have been defined as inferior might realize that they have been told a lie and that they can excel and accomplish extraordinary things if they believe and live according to that belief.

It is our earnest prayer that this book retells part of the narrative of the United States of America. History books do not tell this story. We would like nothing better than to see this story folded into the history of the USA. Yes, we would not mind if media entertainment included this story and others like it to offset the stereotypes that serve all too often as education for the American public.

We encourage institutions, governments, and the church to open their ears to the many voices that have tried for centuries to tell the truth about Africans who were involuntarily settled in this nation but who have embraced it as their own. *Manuel Strong* is only one more story on the mountain of others, but it comes at such a time as this—a time in which America and much of the world is facing a reckoning to confront the horrors of the past and their lasting effects. Amends start in hearts and minds. May the truth help us all toward the healing that starts in thoughts and feelings and flows out to the full extent of our society.

INDEX

school
    public and private 35
second
    job 29
segregated 4
Sensations
    singing group 50
Shari
    in SCC with Nancy 79
Shari Eubanks
    in Emerging Generations 141
Shari Renee
    birth 33
shed
    built by James 22
Sheena
    craftsperson 85
Sheena Virginia 23
Sheree Wilson
    in Emerging Generations 153
Sherman
    dragging home a Christmas
        tree 30
    service to community 86
Sherman Douglas 23
Sinclair Community College 79
skating 50
slavery xii
Spence's Pharmacy 18
sports in Urbana High School 50
Springfield High School 11, 35
Springfield, Ohio 2
Springfield plant 29
Springfield South High School 35
Springfield's Rosedale area 4
Springfield Tigers 14
STAN Solutions
    owned by Tony 87
stereotype xi

stereotypical history xiii
Steve Williamson 44
St. Joseph Catholic School 36
St. Joseph's Catholic Church 4
St. Raphael Catholic School 35
Street Repair
    Springfield 30
Sunday afternoon
    rides in the car 27

T

Theresa Annette 34
third job 29
Tomiko Brown-Nagin 18
Tony 23
    contractor 86
train 18
training their children 22
train to Cincinnati 4
Trash Collection Department 31
Trump's policies xi
Tyler Cudney
    in Emerging Generations 140
Tyrin Alston
    in Emerging Generations 138
Tyrin Raynetta 34

U

UCLA Hospital 60
Up from Slavery xii
Urbana
    mark left on it 58
Urbana High School
    graduates 52
Urbana Ohio
    new home in 1966 37
U.S. Army 58

V

Valerie Harris
    marriage with Greg 56
virtual sports complex
    at the farm 49

W

walkout at the high school 50
Water Street 11
Wheldon Park 14
Wimp family 1
WLAC Nashville 15
work ethic 25
Works Progress Administration
        (WPA) 13
WWII 14

Y

youthful appearance
    inherited from Florine 92

Z

Zeola
    Manuel 4